M000188382

THE VOICE OF
LIVERPOOL
BUSINESS:

The First Chamber of Commerce and the Atlantic Economy

1774 – c.1796

Robert J Bennett MA PhD FBA

1850
LIVERPOOL
CHAMBER *of*
COMMERCE
160 YEARS
2010

The Voice of Liverpool Business

Written by Robert J. Bennett
Graphic design by Ken Ashcroft
Publishing consultant: Fiona Shaw
Proofreading by Judy Tasker
Printed and bound in Spain by Graficas

ISBN: 978-0-9566531-0-9

First published in October 2010 by Liverpool Chamber of Commerce
1 Old Hall Street, Liverpool L3 9HG
www.liverpoolchamber.org.uk

Foreword

The modern Liverpool Chamber of Commerce celebrates 160 years of existence in 2010 and continues to offer a wide-ranging and complex bundle of services to its members and to the local community.

The business has evolved during those 160 years and now helps support individual businesses with information, training and advice; offers networks of opportunity through meetings between groups of businesses; and links the business community to the wider economy. The chamber is also an important partner with local government, national government and regional agencies in the North West for the delivery of public policies and programmes. Liverpool is one of the largest and most prominent of the modern chambers with more than 1,600 members.

A distinctive feature of all the modern UK chambers is their wide service focus. However, this breadth of services has been a relatively recent development - from the last 100 years or so!

The key aspect of the chamber's activity from the very beginning has been to represent members' interests. The earliest chambers all originated in giving a voice to the businesses in their localities; a voice that sought to explain local needs and lobby for changes from government and other agents. In this respect chambers remain essentially as they always have been. They also remain the same in terms of their governance: as voluntary bodies that depend on their members' loyalty, willingness to give time to form 'a chamber view', and to pay subscriptions.

Modern assessments of the motives for chamber membership certainly demonstrate a demand for opportunities to meet, network and market the individuals who own or manage businesses; and gain access to business improvement services. But there is also a commitment to support the actions of the chamber to promote and assist the wider local community, demonstrated by the recent transformation of the chamber into a Community Interest Company.

These motives tend to be held simultaneously. Members retain membership because it offers direct business benefits, but also because they welcome the opportunity to support a valuable cause. As the chamber's influence continues to spread both domestically and internationally, this book provides a fascinating insight into the first Chamber of Commerce in Liverpool, which preceded our own by three-quarters of a century, yet in many ways remained true to the goals and objectives of the modern chamber.

Then, as now, local networking, international trade and overseas business was a fundamental ingredient in the chamber's contribution to the city and is a remarkable example of the adage that the more things change, the more they stay the same.

Contents

The Voice of Liverpool Business: the first Chamber of Commerce 1774 – c.1796

Robert J Bennett

Professor Robert Bennett is an international expert on small businesses and business associations. He was commissioned by the national association, British Chambers of Commerce, to provide their Development Strategy in 1990. The Voice of Liverpool Business is a detailed development of part of his research on the history of chambers, which is to be published by Oxford University Press in 2011. Professor of Georaphy at Cambridge University, he was formerly at the London School of Economics and has held visiting positions in America, Australia and Europe. He has been advisor to various Parliamentary Committees and organisations in the public and private sectors.

Robert J Bennett MA PhD FBA
Professor of Geography
University of Cambridge
Downing Place
Cambridge
CB2 3EN
UK
Email: rjb7@cam.ac.uk

1
The First Liverpool Chamber of Commerce

Introduction

The Liverpool chamber of commerce, founded in 1774, was one of the first in the world, and the earliest UK mainland chamber in a major port. It became an active body over a period of about 20 years, but then fell into abeyance some time between 1792 and 1796. Its story, like that of Liverpool itself, is complex and multi-layered, involving personality, anger, intrigue and conflict. But running across this complexity was a dominant collective concern by its members with their businesses and the economic welfare of the city. Strikingly, many of the issues that engaged the first chamber still worry modern chamber members over 200 years later:

- Economic promotion of the city and region, now through such schemes as Atlantic Gateway
- The costs of the port, as with the recent crisis of revaluation of non-domestic rates on port businesses
- The quality and costs of the postal service and other communications

- Exerting influence to improve government policies on trade and the economy
- Improving the design and enforcement of regulations, such as those over Customs.

These issues engaged the forebears of the modern chamber; and it was outright rage and indignation about some of them that sparked the chamber's first establishment in 1774.

But Liverpool was not alone. Its chamber foundation was part of the first thrust of an experiment with a new model of business organisation: to establish a stable new voice for the local community that could transmit an ordered and unified local business view to others – primarily to government. The chambers of commerce of the English-speaking world began in the 1760s and are the oldest surviving business organisations. The first chamber of commerce was founded in Jersey in 1768; probably the second was in Guernsey in 1769, followed by Manchester in April 1774, and then Liverpool, making it the third or fourth oldest. There were also other early chambers in New York in 1768 and Charleston in late 1773. A Dublin Committee of Merchants, established in 1760, was a body closely resembling a chamber, and this merged with the chamber in 1783. These early chambers were quite distinct in time from a second phase of foundations, which occurred in Glasgow, Birmingham, Belfast, and Dublin in 1783, and Edinburgh and Leeds in 1785. Subsequent development spread the chamber concept across the English-speaking world, and beyond, to create the international brand that is the modern chamber of commerce.

The significance of the first Liverpool chamber of commerce

Liverpool was pivotal in early chamber of commerce development. The more general history of developments across the Atlantic world demonstrates that Liverpool was one of the earliest chambers successfully to overcome the inherent tensions of an independent, voluntary body that was seeking to provide a sustained unity of viewpoint. It was the traffic of communications from the chamber amongst government papers that first drew attention to its significant role.[1] It had the largest scale of correspondence of any chamber with government over 1774–83; it was the most successful in its early years in sustaining a balanced local unity of views in the face of wide diversity of opinion; it was an early experimenter with partnerships to develop other services (such

[1] Information on the general historical evolution of chambers of commerce is derived from the author's large-scale study: Bennett, 2011.

as a newsroom and hotel); and it overcame the strongest competition from other local interests that sought to squash it. Its founding members certainly had great spirit, innovative capacity, commitment and fortitude.

Its history also demonstrates its significant involvement, with others, in national politics in the fraught period leading up to the American rebellion in 1775 and the Declaration of Independence in 1776. The chamber lobbied for caution and conciliation in dealing with the Americans, but its members became divided between seeking peace and war. During and after hostilities, it sought a mutual rapprochement over outstanding debts on both sides, leading up to the 1795 Treaty of Amity. The Atlantic economy ran as a continuing thread through almost all its deliberations.

Yet despite the pivotal local role of Liverpool's chamber and its significance in national political developments, there has been no record or account of it. This book fills that gap. The gap is significant since many of its activities offer important reflections on the development of the city, the national evolution of business activity in this period, the American rebellion, and the emergence of the chambers of commerce as a whole.

This book charts the history through a multi-layered account, building up the detail of its story in what was (and still is) a large and complex city. First, it outlines the challenges of reconstructing the chamber's story from fragmentary records. It then moves, in Chapter 2, to understand what the chamber did. Chapter 3 assesses how it was established and governed. Chapters 4 to 8 then examine the issues that the chamber voiced to government and others.

Seeking a new voice challenged other voices. This involved personalities and pre-existing institutions. Chapters 9–12 assess the different layers of the challenge. Chapter 9 shows that conflicts with the Corporation of Liverpool are critical to understanding why the chamber was formed then, in 1774.

The following chapters seek to unravel the varied layers of membership concerns and how they were networked with each other: in Chapter 10 the members and their characteristics; in Chapter 11 the economic, social and religious networks between the members; and in Chapter 12 the political alignment of the members and their relation to the rest of the city. Chapter 13 assesses why the chamber went into abeyance sometime in 1792–6.

Businesses in this period were personal affairs. There was no general method of incorporation so that businesses were generally either sole traders or partnerships. Most of the Liverpool chamber members were involved in numerous partnerships. This brought social and family relationships into play: to train apprentices, to find partners, to secure inheritance and continuation of the business through appropriate marriages, and to develop networks for assembly of supplies, credit and marketing. Business networks, credit and banking, social networks, religion and politics interweave in the story of the Liverpool chamber. This personal dimension encouraged obligation and mutual support, but also opened scope for conflict and animosity. As we shall see, the history of the first chamber was intimately interlocked with the history of the families involved, and how they related to other families across the city and region.

Lost history

Although Liverpool had one of the very first and most significant early chambers, its history has not been previously systematically analysed nor its importance recognised. The existence of the chamber has been noted in the major 19th century studies of Liverpool by Baines and Brooke, but neither goes further than listing the chamber's committee, respectively, for the years 1774 and 1775.[2] The two 'official' histories of the Liverpool chamber were unaware of the 18th century body, and it is also omitted from the official history of the Association of British Chambers of Commerce.[3] Several widely used early histories of Liverpool institutions written by former Corporation staff ignore the chamber, and tend to over-emphasise the role of government.[4] Some government documents list chamber correspondence solely under 'merchants of Liverpool', rather than explicitly by the chamber; eg in the *Journal of the Committee of Trade and Plantations*. There have also been misunderstandings: for example, Redford's otherwise excellent study of Manchester, which many others have followed, states quite incorrectly that "no general Chamber of Commerce was formed at Liverpool until 1849". Some references substitute the Corporation's committee of trade for the chamber or confuse the two.[5]

---

[2] Baines, 1852, pp 444–5; Brooke, 1853, p 232; Hughes, 1906, uses these as a source for linking some members to early Liverpool banks, and there is also note of chamber membership in some biographies.
[3] Gilson Martin, 1950; Liverpool Chamber of Commerce, 1997; in Ilersic and Liddle, 1960, mention of Liverpool's foundation in 1774 in an Appendix.
[4] Eg Picton, 1886, 1903; Touzeau, 1910.
[5] Redford, 1934, p 19, also p 55; see also Picton, 1886, p 238; Checkland, 1952, p 58–9; Barker and Harris, 1959, p 37.

Re-discovering the lost history

It is understandable that Liverpool's first chamber has been previously largely unrecognised, since few formal records now exist. However, two of its earliest documents have recently re-emerged. First, there is an *Abstract of the proceedings and resolutions of the several committees of the chamber of commerce for the port of Liverpool*, which covers the period 1774–7.[6] Second, there is a draft *Deed*, which formally established the chamber, and specifies its form of organisation and governance: *Draft of an Article, for settling a chamber of commerce in Liverpool, 21st April 1774*.[7]

Unfortunately, there appear to be no surviving personal reflections on the chamber by the members themselves. But an important source is a small collection of papers made by one of the chamber's leading members: Benjamin Heywood, the first treasurer of the chamber, and

Draft article to establish the chamber, 1774

[6] Hereafter referred to as *Abstract*. This appears to exist in only two copies, one at the Library Company of Philadelphia (Am.1777.Liv/log.2251.O.11), and a second at the Athenaeum Library in Liverpool (Misc Pamphlets Vol. LXV). It has been previously referred to by only one other author, Checkland 1952, who did not respond to its significance.

[7] Hereafter referred to as *Deed*. There are two copies of this, one at LRO Holt Gregson papers 942 HOL/10 pp 355–6; the second is at the Liverpool Athenaeum, Gladstone MS no 52, within a collection of Benjamin Heywood's *Calculation and Curious Papers*, of November 1772 ff, hereafter *Heywood Papers*.

a member throughout its existence. Heywood's *Calculations and Curious Papers*, which date from the years following 1772, and contain a copy of the *Deed*, are the closest thing we have to a personal account. These papers are important in showing both Heywood's concerns and those political issues that most angered the chamber's members.

In addition, for 12 years, there are reports of the elections of members of the chamber's committee in local newspapers, which allow many of its leading members to be identified. There is also the correspondence of the chamber with government ministers and others. These sources can be used to reconstruct its lost history. Starting with the names of the committee of the chamber listed in local newspapers, it is possible to undertake a systematic sweep of local newspapers, personal archives, The National Archives (TNA), British Library (BL), Liverpool Record Office (LRO), Liverpool Athenaeum, on-line sources of 18th century literature, local directories, and the records of other contemporary chambers and other organisations corresponding with the Liverpool chamber. The records of the Glasgow chamber of commerce after 1783, and the Bristol Society of Merchant Venturers (SMV) are particularly valuable.

With this approach it is believed that the coverage given here is as complete as possible at the time of writing. However, doubtless more references will be discovered, and the chamber's minute book and accounts, which seem to have been kept, are still to be discovered. Hence, this book may represent only a first attempt at a difficult topic.

2
Objectives of the Chamber

Because of the absence of most formal and personal records, we have limited knowledge of the objectives of the chamber. The *Deed* does not state general objectives, as in other chambers, which usually have statements such as the promotion of "well-being of trade" or "encouragement of trade in this town and its neighbourhood", as in the founding articles used in the earlier Jersey and Manchester chambers, respectively. Instead Liverpool's *Deed* begins with the statement that "Common utility, mutual wants, and the necessity of mutual services, gave rise to an ancient association in Liverpool, for the levying of a small tax, under denomination of a trade duty. ... To give stability to that trade, in its now extended state, requires an increase of attention, and an increase of public expense. Therefore we whose names are hereunto subscribed, merchants and tradesmen, within the port of Liverpool ... being fully convinced of the real necessity of raising a fund for the public support of commercial interests of this port; and that the most effectual method of establishing a capital for that purpose, will be by an annual payment of such sums, as the merchants and tradesmen of this port may think proper to subscribe."

The key founding concern of the chamber was, therefore, to develop a new 'economic fund' as an alternative or addition to the trade duty then levied by the Corporation. This focus on the trade duty is unique to Liverpool, but as we shall see later, it was critical to generating the energy and commitment of business people to establish the chamber: they were very angry with the Corporation. The rest of the *Deed*, however, gives no further statement of purpose; it lists 13 articles covering procedures. Hence, to understand the chamber's objectives more fully, we have to infer from its only other formal record, the *Abstract*, and its actual activities.

Voice and lobbying

Whatever the concern with the trade duty, the chamber's central activity was that of lobbying: to act as a voice on behalf of businesses in Liverpool, with its target being mainly the Westminster government. The *Abstract* of its activities for its first three years covers almost nothing else. In the years 1774–7 it mounted 34 lobby, petition or representational activities on a wide range of topics. These lobbies continued over the rest of its life up to c 1796. These are the main subject of the rest of this book. But it enlarged its objectives beyond a local voice in four respects.

(i) Regional and national voice

The chamber sought not just to represent Liverpool in a narrow sense but also to represent Liverpool's interests in a regional setting, and in co-ordination with similar local and national interests. Analysis of its known members shows that they were chiefly from Liverpool itself, but also included leading St Helens coal and salt miners/refiners; the Cheshire salt producers; canal proprietors in these two areas; Lancaster merchants; and had some connection with the new Manchester chamber of commerce and that city's businesses. Thus, the Liverpool chamber was acting, sometimes with Manchester, as a regional as well as a local voice.

It was also active nationally. When the state of British interests and debt in America was first formally considered on 29 December 1774, the *Abstract* states "A circular letter was therefore ordered to be transmitted to the principal trading towns, connected with the port, requesting to be informed, whether any, and what measures, were intended to be adopted by each town respectively, upon the alarming state of the commerce between Great Britain and America." Similarly in mid–1775, a letter from Bristol "was read, and supported" proposing a parliamentary petition to seek redress for "suffers by the plundering of shipwrecks".[8] In December 1775, jointly with the city of Chester, negotiation was opened with the manager of a Bill before parliament for the erection of a lighthouse at the Point of Ayr. Similarly a continuing exchange was maintained with the Africa Company, both in Liverpool, and in London and Bristol.[9] These early concerns continued throughout the chamber's life.

The main Bristol connection is particularly significant. This was with the Bristol Society of Merchant Venturers, who frequently acted with Liverpool in this period; they exchanged at least 15 letters with the Liverpool chamber, mainly in 1774–9. Correspondence was also being continually received from informants in America, the West Indies and Africa, as well as nearby ports such as Whitehaven and in Ireland: on trading conditions, enemy activity and privateering.[10] The importance of these exchanges is indicated by the shift in the Bristol correspondence to refer to Liverpool as "the Chamber of Commerce" in its proceedings and index by 1775,[11] indicating that there was no other chamber at this time with which it was in contact. This is further indicated by there being only one recorded exchange of Bristol with the Manchester chamber, and that was through Liverpool. In 1779 the Liverpool chamber sent a letter from the Manchester chamber, which was rebuffed by the Bristol Venturers.[12]

As a result, Liverpool, for a short period in the 1770s, acting in conjunction with the Bristol Venturers and London interests, appears to have become almost a national voice on some issues, in the sense that it represented both the concerns of the city and those national interests on which the city primarily focused: the Atlantic trade with America, Africa and the West Indies, specific taxes, and opposition to various government policies (primarily through its local opposition MPs, though also through local representatives of the government interest if they were supportive). This role filled something of a vacuum after the outbreak of war with America (with the Lexington incident in April 1775), when the former American colonial agents in London either returned or were sidelined, until other chambers and voices emerged over 1783–5.

(ii) Meeting room and the Tontine Hotel (Bates)

An early desire to broaden objectives beyond lobbying is indicated by brief concluding comments in the *Abstract* (pp 15–16). This suggests:

[8] *Abstract*, p 8; this refers to the Bristol SMV. This letter was sent 7 June 1775 to John Dobson via Joseph Dalterra (both chamber members in Liverpool) to alert them to the next "season of business in Parliament": out-letters, SMV/2/4/1. James Dalterra, a Bristol relative of Joseph Dalterra who was a Liverpool chamber member, was a leading member of the SMV and treasurer during the 1780s; a banker in Dalterra and Roche. The family was of Huguenot origin.

[9] *Abstract*, p 12, January 2 1777.

[10] *Abstract*, pp 14–15.

[11] SMV Proceedings: SMV/2/1/1/10; Index SMV/2/1/2/3.

[12] Letter from Gill Slater, President of Liverpool chamber to SMV, sending a memorial from the Committee of Trade of Manufacturers of Manchester, 7 December 1779; out-letters, SMV/2/4/1/1.

"That it would probably tend to general satisfaction, if a room was taken in the neighbourhood of the Exchange, where all the books, and letters of this Society [chamber] should be open to the inspection of the subscribers every day during 'Change hours; and a suitable allowance made to the secretary for the additional care and attendance." This indicates recognition of the benefits of opening topics and correspondence to a broader discourse and assessment by the membership than could be achieved by formal meetings alone: ie to have a 'drop-in' meeting room.

Other early chamber foundations were intimately connected with establishing arenas for exchange of information, chiefly reading rooms. It appears probable that the Liverpool chamber was seeking something of this facility in 1777. Most chamber members (71% of known members - see Appendix Table A.3) were in any case members of the Subscription Library, established in 1758, and clearly sought out opportunities to meet and exchange views. Perhaps the chamber members also had in mind Jersey chamber's regular dining room, or New York, where one of the chamber's founding Articles required a room for conversation with "bread and cheese, beer, punch, pipes and tobacco, provided at the expense of the members present".[13] Liverpool merchants would be aware of these chambers, both established six years earlier, in 1768, through their frequent trading exchanges and visits.

A chamber room does not seem to have been secured immediately. But in 1783–4 a 'Tontine Coffee Room, Hotel and Tavern' was launched by four of the known or probable chamber members, with its accounts held by Arthur Heywood, another member.[14] They were to act as trustees, with rents and profits distributed annually to shareholders. Five thousand guineas was initially sought to finance this scheme. It was very successful, since by 1793 it had accumulated a balance of £9,620 in Heywoods' bank. The building was built on a former timber yard, on the north-east corner of Lord St with Whitechapel, and opened by 1784.[15] When completed it was initially called the New Hotel, then Royal Hotel, and then Bates Hotel. It had a coffee room 80 by 28 feet, which became the main newspaper room of the city, three dining rooms, several smaller rooms and parlours, lodging rooms, kitchen, laundry, brewhouse, rooms for servants, and good cellars. It became 'the first'

---

[13] Bishop, 1918, p 6; see also Bennett, 2011, chapter 12.
[14] Richard Heywood, Thomas Ryan, John Gregson and Gill Slater; launch advertisement in Williamsons Advertiser, 5 June 1783; notices of sale of Tontine shares 4 February 1784 (LRO Holt Gregson papers 942 HOL/8, p 127).
[15] Accounts for the 'Hotel Coffee Room of Thomas Ryan': Heywood Bank ledger 1791–4, Barclays Bank archives pp 97, 110; see also Brooke, 1853, pp 269, 375; Ormerod, 1952.

LIVERPOOL, 14th February, 1784,

The PREMISES in LORD-STREET,

INTENDED FOR

An HOTEL and COFFEE-ROOM,

BEing purchafed by RICHARD HEYWOOD, THOMAS RYAN, JOHN GREGSON, and GILL SLATER, with an Intent to complete the fame for the Accommodation of the Public on a liberal Plan, they have examined the different Eftimates, and find that the fame may be finifhed for about Five Thoufand Pounds, including the Purchafe-Money, amounting to One Thoufand Nine Hundred and Fifty Pounds.

In thefe Eftimates, the Timber Yard, and the Buildings thereon, in the Poffeffion of Mr. EDWARD LOWE, purchafed for the Convenience of the HOTEL, with all the neceffary Offices to be erected thereon, are included, for which laft-mentioned Premifes and Buildings the intended Tenant agrees to allow Seven per Cent. per Annum.

A Plan is agreed upon, and propofed for the Confideration of thofe Gentlemen who wifh to become Subfcribers, which may be feen at the Office of SLATER, CALDWELL, and KENNION, from MONDAY the Sixteenth inftant, to MONDAY the Firft of MARCH, both Days inclufive; and if the prefent Purchafers fhall then find that the Scheme cannot be accomplifhed, according to the faid Plan, it is intended to re-fell the Premifes, of which public Notice will be given.

S C H E M E

For FINISHING the HOTEL and COFFEE-ROOM,

In LORD-STREET,

By TONTINE, with BENEFIT of SURVIVORSHIP,

IN FOUR CLASSES.

TO confift of not lefs than Two Hundred Shares, at Twenty-five Guineas per Share, in order to raife Five Thoufand Guineas, being the Amount of the feveral Eftimates for compleating the Buildings; if the Number of Shares fubfcribed for, fhall exceed Two Hundred, the Value of each Share to decreafe in Proportion.

1ft Clafs, under 20 Years of Age,	}	It is underftood that each Clafs will be eventually
2d	20 to 40	entitled to a Property in the Premifes, according
3d	40 to 50	to the Number of Shares fubfcribed for in that
4th	50 and upwards.	*particular Clafs.*

That no Subfcriber be limited to any Number of Shares.

That the Conveyance of the Premifes being made out in the Names of the Purchafers, Meffrs. RICHARD HEYWOOD, THOMAS RYAN, JOHN GREGSON, and GILL SLATER, they fhall be confidered as Acting Truftees, and make a Divifion of the neat Rents and Profits, which fhall be paid annually, at the Bank of A. HEYWOOD, Efq; Son, and Co. unlefs the Majority of the Subfcribers, at a general Meeting, fhall appoint a Committee for the above Purpofe.

If, by any Error in the Eftimate, more than Five Thoufand Guineas be found neceffary to complete the Premifes, the annual Rent fhall be funk till fuch Deficiency be made good.

Unlefs a fufficient Number of Subfcribers can be procured to raife Five Thoufand Guineas, this Scheme muft be entirely given up.

That a Committee fhall be appointed, for the exprefs Purpofe of regulating the Coffee-Room.

Five Guineas per Share to be depofited at the Time of fubfcribing, and the faid Five Guineas to be returned immediately, in Cafe the Plan does not go forward.

That each Subfcriber fhall name his Life or Lives on or before the Firft of MAY next, otherwife the Life of the Subfcriber muft be confidered as the Life for which fuch Subfcriber intends to hold his Share or Shares.

Advertisement for Tontine hotel (Bates), 1784

of inns, with 'fifty or sixty bedrooms'.[16] Its reading room was the largest available until the Athenaeum.[17]

Bates was not itself a chamber building, since a separate body of subscribers was sought, about 200 in number, both women and men. But its link with the chamber's members was close, since it was where the chamber often met. It became, in effect, a partnership link of the chamber with the initiative of sympathetic members. It was also successful, since Bates became the most frequently used venue for major meetings of the merchants, when petitions and subscription initiatives were raised, until the Exchange was rebuilt in 1802. Bates acted as the city's main newsroom until the Athenaeum was built in 1798, which also had the support of many chamber members when subscriptions were launched in 1797. The chamber members thus seem to have gained a meeting room in 1784, as well as wider facilities, through a partnership effort with its leading members and other subscribers. But it seems unlikely that the chamber had a dedicated room in Bates as occurred in some other chambers. Rather, as in Glasgow, the chamber shared the facilities with general reading and meeting rooms.

(iii) Leader on collective legal actions

A further effort by the chamber was an attempt to fight a legal action related to the Jamaican slave tax. This was introduced in 1774 as a duty of 40 shillings per head upon slaves imported into Jamaica, increased by the Jamaica Assembly in early 1775 to "two pounds ten shillings payable by the importer; and a further duty of five pounds upon every negroe, which at importation shall be reported to be above 30 years of age, by any two of 74 inspectors, to be appointed by the magistrates of the Island; ... with the addition of one shilling a head for every slave examined by the inspectors."[18]

To fight these duties "The Chamber of Commerce at this time offered their service, to conduct the prosecution, necessary for the recovery of the duty ... provided a proportional subscription was entered into by the parties concerned, to defray the expenses of such prosecution." However, "*The want of unanimity in those Gentlemen who had paid the duty, has hitherto prevented any further proceedings in this business*".[19] Hence, an additional activity with additional costs was envisaged, but was not actually developed. This may have been the best

---

[16] Quoted from a visitor to Bates Hotel in 1798; p 31 in Gay, N., 1799; see also Williamson's Advertiser, 5 June 1783.
[17] Troughton, 1810, pp 343–8.
[18] *Abstract*, pp 3, 6; see also Journal of Committee of Trade and Plantations, 1774–7.
[19] *Abstract*, p 5, italics in original.

outcome, since a legal case taken up by the early Manchester chamber in 1796 led to heavy costs being incurred that proved difficult to recover from the parties. It was a probable cause of the demise of that chamber, in 1801, when it appears that the chamber then became insolvent.[20]

(iv) Benevolent activity

A further possible chamber service is listed in the *Deed*, Article 9, which mentions benevolent "assistance and relief" to members arising from "unavoidable misfortune in the course of trade". The lack of records prevents us knowing whether such assistance was given, but if used it could only have been limited given the small resources of the chamber. It could have been invoked with the demise of Caldwell's bank in 1793, since Charles Caldwell was a member. But it is unlikely that this support was developed. However, many of the chamber's members were supporters of the Marine Society when this was launched in Liverpool, in 1789, as a charity to help the dependants of seamen.

Other services

Many early chambers did offer other services; for example arbitration of commercial disputes (offered by New York and Jersey from 1768; and Glasgow, Edinburgh and Dublin in the 1780s), managing letters of marque (as in Jersey and the Dublin Committee of Merchants), running local markets or harbours and quays (in most early Irish chambers), installing navigation lights, and developing private Bills for urban improvements. Manchester and Birmingham were active in protecting patent rights; and Leeds and Manchester became involved in product testing and market regulation.[21] But there is no evidence of these early services in Liverpool, though a possible role in letters of marque is worthy of further research.

It would thus appear that the central objective of the first Liverpool chamber, although focusing in the draft *Deed* on the trade duty, was essentially to lobby and act as a voice. This went further than just Liverpool itself, embracing a range of regional and national trading interests in which Liverpool was involved. A meeting room was desired, and this was indeed developed in the form of the Bates Hotel Tontine by leading chamber members through a wider subscription, but other significant services to members were probably not developed.

---

[20] Manchester chamber of commerce (Society of Commerce) minute book (John Rylands Library); also quoted in Redford, 1934, pp 47–48.
[21] See Bennett, 2011, vhapter 12.

Table 1 The 13 Articles of the Liverpool chamber of commerce founding *Deed;* summarised

Art. 1	To agree to pay an annual subscription for three years on 1 May to the treasurer
Art. 2	To hold an annual meeting on 24 June each year (or if a Sunday on the next day), and elect a committee of 21 members
Art. 3	Each committee member to act as trustee, and sign his agreement in a book; the committee to elect a chair and deputy chair
Art. 4	Committee members to be summoned 48 hours before each meeting, with no less than 11 members able to make expenditure decisions; the chair to have a casting vote in event of equal division of opinion; and all meetings to be held in a public room
Art. 5	Each year seven of the committee will elected by ballot to continue for the succeeding year, and 14 shall retire with new committee members elected from the full chamber's membership
Art. 6	Only those members who have paid their annual subscription of one pound one shilling can vote for committee men and make any claim on the funds of the chamber
Art. 7	Once subscriptions in any year have reached £100, this is placed out at interest, with the committee as trustees
Art. 8	No new subscriber will be admitted after 24 January 1775
Art. 9	Assistance to any subscriber can be given at discretion of the committee of at least 11 members
Art. 10	The committee should meet on the first Thursday of each month between 10.00 and 12.00; the chair, or deputy in his absence, can call occasional meetings with less than 48 hours' notice in emergencies, but cannot make expenditure decisions
Art. 11	The committee will choose a clerk and settle his salary. The clerk will keep books in the committee room of all orders and resolutions and account for all monies
Art. 12	The annual accounts to be printed and published and sent to each subscriber on 24 June
Art. 13	Any person paying twenty guineas or more will become a benefactor and have the privileges of an annual subscriber

3
Establishment, governance and organisation

In terms of formal governance the draft *Deed* appears accurately to describe the way the chamber operated in almost all instances. It contained 13 Articles of governance, summarised in Table 1.

Establishment

The *Deed* was printed and distributed on 21 April 1774. There was then a delay whilst subscribers were solicited, with election of the first committee and chair in June, but the subscription list remained open until 24 January 1775. The purpose of the *Deed* was a statement to which subscribers, by signing, agreed to the specified mode of governance and management of the funds raised. A subscription list would be left in one or several locations, usually coffee houses, for supporters to sign. Liverpool's *Deed* was left at John Gore's bookshop from April until June, when an open advertisement appeared for "subscribers to the chamber of commerce [are requested] to meet at Pontack's Coffee House at 10.00 [on 24 June] in order to elect the committee for the ensuing year. In the meantime those who chose to encourage so laudable an undertaking may see the deed by applying to John Gore".[22]

---

[22] Advertisement in Williamsons Advertiser, and Gore's General Advertiser, 17 and 24 June 1774; Gore was a prominent bookseller and stationer at the time, although there is no evidence that he was a member of chamber.

There was no general mechanism for incorporation as a limited liability company at this time, so that many organisations and societies sought formal establishment through a legal document, which, in effect, provided for a common law partnership of the subscribers, with a partnership Deed. The only alternative would be trusts, as with canals and turnpikes. The partnership would be most familiar from the daily commercial life of Liverpool merchants, and was also the model used for establishing numerous other 'public' institutions, for example the Subscription Library set up in Liverpool in 1758 (later called the Lyceum). Through the Deed a group of 'subscribers' put up an initial capital sum subject to a set of rules, which defined it as a legal form. No further payments might be necessary, since the capital itself assured the continued status of the body and a flow of interest income. But further income was usually sought from an annual subscription to fund current expenditures, the initial capital remaining as an endowment.

A partnership for a period

In Liverpool the draft *Deed* shows that the chamber was established initially for three years: "We the several subscribers hereto, do promise and engage, in order that the scheme may have a fair trial, we will severally continue to pay our respective annual subscriptions, for the term of three years certain, the first payment whereof, to be made on the first day of May next, and so on the first day of May, for the two succeeding years, to Mr Arthur Heywood who is hereby appointed Treasurer" (Art. 1). This was a limited legal deed of obligation. As a result of its form, after three years it would be necessary to re-launch the chamber and define a new set of subscription obligations. This explains why the *Abstract* exists: it was a document to seek renewed support after the first three-year period. Hence, the *Abstract* (p 20) opines, at the 1777 Annual Meeting: "That a continuation of subscriptions, limited in amount at the option of the subscriber, under such regulations as may hereafter be agreed upon, is essentially necessary."

Arthur Heywood, 1717-95

The three-year subscription model used by Liverpool is remarkable for its resemblance to that used in Jersey at its foundation six years earlier in 1768. Moreover these are the only two chambers definitely to use this model (although it is probable that Manchester also used it over 1774–81). This may suggest that a copy of Jersey's Articles was available in Liverpool. Jersey's founding Article 14 states that "each subscription is to be for three years certain". This led to a process by which the chamber had to be dissolved by revoking the previous agreement (allowing members to retrieve their capital), and reconstituted at the end of each three-year period, with the new subscribers then forming a new shareholding membership. In the case of Jersey, once one half of the stock was subscribed, it was placed in annuities in London in the name of the president, who entered into a bond with the chamber for the value of the stock. The whole model was more akin to a debenture than the sort of annual subscriptions that are familiar today.

In Liverpool the three-year model appears to have been abandoned in 1777 in favour of the annual subscription model. The capital raised, once £100 had been subscribed, was to be placed out on a low or moderate interest in the names of the committee who declared by deed, bond, bill, or note that the money is the property of the chamber and that the names act on trust for the chamber (Art. 7) – an identical style of trust to that in Jersey.

Subscriptions and the use of the trade duty

The subscription structure envisaged is another resonance with the Jersey chamber. As noted above, originally the Liverpool *Deed* specified subscriptions as a levy like the trade duty, though it was clearly set at a voluntary level more as a capital gift or debenture. Jersey had instituted its initial subscriptions as a direct trade duty "of 3d Sterling per ton per annum … upon the tonnage belonging to each respective member …, measured at the direction of the committee", with a different levy for non-shipping businesses based on the scale of the business.[23] The overlap of these two concepts (three-year shareholders and trade duty) suggest the transfer of the Jersey experience to Liverpool, though the language used, and the order of articles in the two chambers' Deeds suggests that Liverpool did not possess a copy of the Jersey Articles, but received information by word of mouth.[24]

---

[23] Jersey chamber minutes, founding Articles no 13, L/A/38/A1/1; Jersey Archives.
[24] The Liverpool-American chamber in 1811–60 also financed itself by a trade duty on imports of members collected by Customs officials; Minutes, LRO 380 AME/4; Henderson, 1933a.

The subscription lists unfortunately have not survived.[25] The *Deed* suggests that the sums varied in a voluntary fashion, but after the initial capital was established, the subscription was "one pound one shilling ... or upwards" (Art. 6). This was clearly adequate since the same sum was maintained: the concluding statement of the *Abstract* states that it had been agreed at the 1777 Annual Meeting:[26] "That it would be a liberal and useful regulation, to admit any Gentleman a member of this Society, upon payment of such sum as may be hereafter agreed on to the present fund [ie the capital fund], and an annual subscription of not less than one guinea a year." This confirms that in the first three years the chamber was a 'closed' membership of its initial subscribers, closed on 24 January 1775 (Art. 8). But from mid-1777 membership was re-opened to new members, who were to pay similar capital sums to those of the initial subscribers, and thereafter an annual subscription.

Whilst the initial capital subscription is not quoted, the *Deed* in its final Article offered the opportunity that to become a benefactor (Art. 13); ie they became a hybrid of shareholder and life member. This suggests that the initial subscription was 20 guineas which, with an estimated 150 members (qv below), indicates a start-up capital of about £3,000. This is comparable with Glasgow and Edinburgh chambers, which in 1783 both used 10 guineas as an initial and life fee, Manchester in 1774 probably had a 20 guinea fee, and Waterford had a debenture structure ranging from £10 to £50 in 1797.[27] Thus the Liverpool chamber was using a subscription levy common at the time, with the initial three-year shareholder model seemingly borrowed from Jersey, but then abandoned in 1777.

Governing committee

Concerning formal governance, the *Deed* provided that at annual meetings on 24 June each year, those present would elect a committee of 21 members (Art. 2), who in turn would elect the officers of a chairman and vice chairman (Art. 3). All committee members were voluntary, and none received an honorarium. The formal election results for the chamber's committee and holding of annual meetings were precisely reported in the local newspapers.

---

[25] The Treasurer, Arthur Heywood, should have had such a list, but this is not in his papers at the Barclays bank archives. A check of all the other successor banks also reveals no financial records for the chamber held by others. Also none of the personal papers and account books consulted show records of personal payment to the chamber (eg LRO: Staniforth, Tarleton, Leyland, Holt Gregson, Bostock papers; Merseyside Maritime Museum: Cropper, Davenport, Earle papers; Flintshire RO: Gladstone papers; William Clement Library Michigan: Charles Goore letterbook).

[26] *Abstract*, p 16.

[27] Glasgow and Edinburgh Minute Books and Annual Accounts; Manchester, reported in *The London Magazine on Gentlemen's Monthly Intelligencer*, Vol. XLIII, 1774, p 502; Waterford Minute Book and Accounts; Bennett, 2011.

As in other voluntary associations, the committee became the core group who took on all the legal responsibilities and liabilities of the organisation. Thus the *Deed* explicitly defines how each committee member acknowledges their legal position (Art. 3): "every committee-man shall acknowledge his acceptance of the trust, within three days after his appointment, and notice given him, by subscribing his name in a book to be kept for that purpose".

The elections were held regularly and reported from 1774/5 until 1786/7, but with no report for 1784/5, and no reports after 1786/7. At these "annual meetings of the subscribers" the *Deed* (Art. 5) provided that one-third (7) of the members continued each year and two-thirds (14) retired. In the newspapers it is reported that this was "agreeable to the annual custom".[28] However, up to 1780 only seven retired each year. From 1780 the process reverted to that stated in the Deed, and it is reported explicitly that "seven from the former committee and 14 subscribers not on last year's committee" were elected.[29] This implies some discord in that year and a pressure to revert to the formal *Deed* in order to increase the turnover of the committee.

This model of governance demonstrates the strong grassroots base of the early chamber. Whilst the elected committee was delegated to

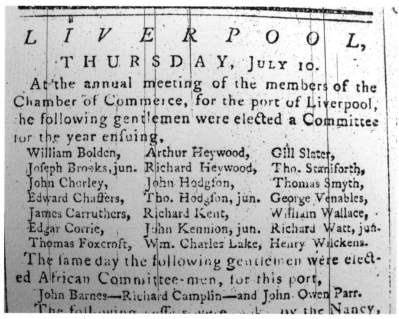

Newspaper advertisement for chamber AGM, 1782

[28] Eg Williamsons Advertiser 25 June 1779, et seq.
[29] Williamsons Advertiser 29 June 1780; 26 June 1781.

take action on behalf of the members, it was desired that they held this mandate for only a short time, and that all major decisions were referred back to the whole membership through general meetings at which the chamber's policy position would be discussed and agreed. In practice, however, it was inevitable then, as now, that much of the activity fell on the shoulders of the committee, and especially its secretary, who became the leading facilitator of the whole enterprise.

The committee members

The full list of membership of the committee of the chamber, currently known, is shown in Table 2 for elections 1774–87. These become the main dramatis personae for the rest of this book!

Table 2 shows some effect of the move in 1780 for 14 members (two-thirds) to retire each year. Clearly some members at this time felt that there was a need for greater turnover. Certainly prior to 1780 a relatively small group had dominated the chamber: 16 members had served on the committee for five of the six years; and nine of these had served for all six years (Brooks, Chaffers, Chorley, Kent, Nottingham, Rawlinson, Slater, Smythe and Staniforth). These nine, with the addition of the other seven serving for five years, formed the core of the early chamber (Ashton, Bolden, Dobson, Foxcroft, Heywood, Venables and Wallace). From 1780, many of this core group continued, despite the new rotation: seven (Brooks, Chaffers, Chorley, Kent, Slater, Staniforth and Watt) served for at least four of the next six years where there are records. In total, for the 12 years with records, there were only 61 committee members (whereas there could have been 245: 252 minus the 7 who remained from the first year), and the same secretary, Samuel Green, served for 18 years from 1774 until his death in 1792. Hence it is clear that the chamber was primarily run by a core group of 20–30 key members, most of whom were involved from the outset.

Chairman and vice chairman

The *Deed* provided for the committee to elect its chair and vice chair annually. Unfortunately, we do not have complete records of who filled these posts, but a summary of known chairs is given in Appendix Table A.1. The records confirm that John Dobson was chair in at least two of the early years (1774–5 and 1776–7) and other information also shows he was a prime early mover. Gill Slater was chair in at least five years (1777–8 to 1779–80, and 1781–2 to 1783–4). Vice chairs were Thomas Smythe in 1774–5, and Thomas Staniforth in 1777–8 and 1781–2. These

Table 2. Members of the committee of the Liverpool Chamber of Commerce 1774–96, from midsummer each year until the following year. (Sources: Liverpool Williamson's Advertiser; Gore's General Advertiser; Gore's Directory for 1781; and materials quoted in the text; no reported information for 1784–5 or after 1786–7). Note: differs from listing of first two years in Baines (1852) and Brooke (1853) for some initials, after correction from primary sources; the secretary is not a member of the committee of 21.

Name	74–5	75–6	76–7	77–8	78–9	79–80	80–1	81–2	82–3	83–4	85–6	86–7
John Armstrong								•				
Nicholas Ashton	•	•	•		•	•			•			
Robert Bent												•
William Bolden		•	•	•	•	•	•	•		•	•	
John Bolton												•
Joseph Brooks jun	•	•	•	•	•	•		•	•	•	•	•
Charles Caldwell							•		•			•
James Carruthers							•		•	•		
Thomas Case	•	•	•	•								
Edward Chaffers	•	•	•	•	•	•	•	•		•	•	
John Chorley	•	•	•	•	•	•	•		•	•	•	
John Copland									•			
Edgar Corrie		•	•		•	•				•		
Joseph Dalterra	•			•			•					
John Dobson	•	•	•	•		•	•	•				•
George Dunbar												•
William Earle	•											
Edward Falkner								•				
Thomas Falkner	•	•			•							
John Fisher								•			•	•
Joseph Fowden							•					
Thomas Foxcroft	•		•	•	•	•		•		•		
Samuel Halliday						•						
Stephen Hayes												•
Arthur Heywood	•	•	•		•	•	•		•			•
Benjamin Heywood	•						•		•		•	
Richard Heywood							•		•			•
John Hodgson			•	•	•		•			•	•	•
Thomas Hodgson		•			•		•					
Thomas Hodson jun		•		•	•	•		•	•	•		•
Francis Ingram	•	•				•						
William James	•	•										

Table 2 continued

Name	74–5	75–6	76–7	77–8	78–9	79–80	80–1	81–2	82–3	83–4	85–6	86–7
John Kennion jun							•		•			
Richard Kent	•	•	•	•	•	•		•	•	•	•	•
Thomas Lake			•	•			•		•		•	
William Charles Lake							•		•		•	
Joseph Leay									•			
Hugh Hindley Leigh			•	•								
Thomas Leyland							•		•		•	
Thomas Manley												•
Edward Mason							•					
Arnold Meyer							•		•			
John Meyers							•		•			
Matthew Nicholson							•					
Alexander Nottingham	•	•	•	•	•	•						
Joseph Rathbone							•					
Thos. Henry Rawlinson	•	•	•	•	•	•	•					
Thomas Rawson											•	
Thomas Ryan							•		•			•
Gill Slater	•	•	•	•	•	•	•	•	•	•	•	•
Thomas Smythe	•	•	•	•	•	•		•		•	•	
Thomas Staniforth	•	•	•	•	•	•	•	•	•	•	•	•
John Tarleton											•	
Thomas Tarleton		•	•				•	•	•			
Tyzack Trotter					•							
George Venables	•	•	•	•	•		•		•	•	•	
Paul Wagner									•			
William Wallace	•		•	•	•		•		•	•	•	
Richard Watt jun				•	•	•		•	•	•	•	
Henry Wilckens									•			
Samuel Green (Sec. up to 1792)	•	•	•	•	•	•	•	•	•	•	•	•

four were thus the key early leaders of the chamber. There is possible circumstantial evidence that other chairs or vice chairs were Henry Wilckens in 1787–8, probably again in 1788–9; and Edgar Corrie in 1790–1 and 1791–2 (see later below). Perhaps John Tarleton took a role as quasi chair after 1793. From this record it appears that the chair probably held office for three- to four-year periods, though the *Deed* does not state any limits on tenure.

The secretary

The committee chose a secretary, or clerk, who "was employed under them", and paid an annual salary (*Deed*, Art. 11). He kept the books and was additional to the committee, and thus we must assume was not able to vote. His salary was probably a nominal annual honorarium of about £30–50 in line with other contemporary chambers; in Jersey it was 32 *Livres*.[30] The Liverpool secretary also had to provide a security for his good conduct of £500 "for the faithful discharge and perform-ance of the trust committed to him". This implies that the individual had to be reasonably prosperous, or had connections that were able to secure this sort of sum. In fact the man appointed, Samuel Green, was an established merchant in the Irish linen trade who would have been undertaking the task as only a part of his activity and may not have been paid. The *Deed* also specified that the annual accounts of the chamber should be printed and published annually and delivered to each subscriber on each 24 June (Art. 12); however, only the *Abstract*, but no accounts, appears to have been published or survived.

For the 12 years fully covered in Table 2, therefore, we have firm evidence of a formalised structure with regular elections, a formal secre-tary, with a group of key players managing the chamber's business, regular general and monthly meetings,[31] and active lobbying on a variety of issues of importance to Liverpool and its trade. The opening to new members on an annual basis from 1777 demonstrates the chamber's concern to widen its membership and move away from the closed three-yearly subscription model. The shift in electoral structure of the committee in 1780 demonstrates response to some form of grassroots feelings, but the re-emergence of the old guard suggests that either few members were willing to take on the burdens of the chamber's committee meetings and obligations, or the old guard were entrenched.

---

[30] Jersey chamber minutes; Brooke, 1853, p 115, states that a clerk in Liverpool was paid £30 per year in 1776–8.

[31] The *Deed*, Article 10, required monthly meetings; only the annual meetings are reported in the newspapers.

4
Early voice and lobbying activities: 1774–7

As noted above, the central activity of the first Liverpool chamber of commerce, like all the other early chambers, was acting as a local voice to lobby government and its administrative departments. From the full record of its activities 1774–7, and the more fragmentary evidence for later periods, we can obtain a reasonably complete picture of the main concerns of the Liverpool business community represented by the chamber. In the *Abstract*, 35 lobby, petition or representational activities are recorded for the three years 1774–7. This is a high level of activity by contemporary or even modern standards: Liverpool had a very active new lobbying body.[32] It can also be supplemented with other material from other sources.

An analysis of the main targets of the lobbies, their success, and the field of trade involved over 1774–7 is shown in Table 3. The lobbying was primarily concerned with international trade; this was 23 (65.7%) of the lobbies mounted. National issues were also important, however, covering six (17.1%) of the lobbies. Purely local issues were also the concern of six lobbies (17.1%), though only one was a lobby on local institutions; all the rest concerned the treatment of Liverpool by national bodies.

[32] The list is considerably more extensive than that attributed to the *Abstract* by Checkland, 1952, pp 58–9, who lists only three lobbies, two of which were by a Corporation Committee not the chamber.

A N

A B S T R A C T

OF THE

PROCEEDINGS and RESOLUTIONS

OF THE

Several C O M M I T T E E S

OF THE

Chamber of Commerce

FOR THE

PORT of *LIVERPOOL,*

From their Firſt Eſtabliſhment on the 24th *June,* 1774,

To the 24th *June,* 1777,

Is humbly ſubmitted to the Public, as the trueſt teſt of the uſefulneſs of this inſtitution, and the faireſt foundation for a judgment, how far it is deſerving of further ſupport.

The abstract of the chamber's first three years

International issues

Of the international issues, most were related to the effect of the emerging American war on trade: ten involved convoys, privateering and protection of shipping; five involved embargoes on arms, provisions or other trading; and two related to trade and debt in America. But other issues were also important: three concerned the slave tax imposed by Jamaica; and one each related to the Greenland fishing bounty, unfair trading, and forts in the Gold Coast.

The evidence of the *Abstract* for 28 May 1777 is supplemented by a letter from John Dobson as chair of the chamber to the Merchant Venturers in Bristol asking for their support in petitioning parliament about American privateering with French and Spanish crews.[33] Bristol also wrote to Dobson earlier in 1777 criticising the Africa Company's management of forts in Africa and asking for support.[34] There is also an exchange of several letters over late 1776 and early 1777 of Dobson and

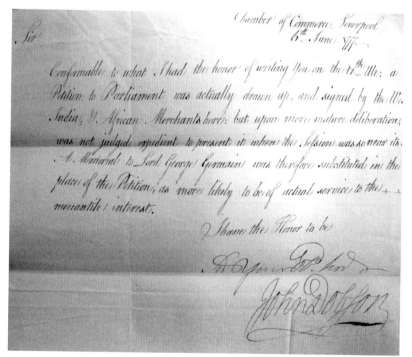

Letter from chamber president John Dobson, 1777

---

[33] Dobson letters to SMV 28 May and 6 June, 1777; SMV/2/4/2/20 (13); and quoted in Proceedings 14 June 1777, SMV/2/1/1/10; see also *The Remembrancer*, London, 1784, letter printed in full on pp 142–3.

[34] Dobson to SMV 4 April 1777, SMV/2/4/2/20 (8); SMV out-letters 17 February 1777: SMV/2/4/1/1. The Corporation was also involved in reporting on the African forts: Journal of the Committee for Trade and Plantations, 21 and 28 February, and 3 March 1777.

Table 3 Lobbying activity of Liverpool Chamber of Commerce 1774–1777, with levels of success, targets and field of trade affected (tabulation of reports and self-assessment in *Abstract*, 1777, pp 3–15; other known activities reported in the text are not included); the dates show the chamber years, from 24 June, and the calendar years

Date	Lobby topic	Target of lobby	Self-assessment of success (Y/N)	Field: local	Field: national	Field: international
1774/5	Timing of postal service	PO	N	•		
	Slave tax at Jamaica	Minister	N			•
	Corn law	Gov. Pownall	N		•	
	American property and debts	Parliament	N			•
1775	Port landwaiters, porters, scales	Treasury	Y	•		
	Trade conditions with America, Africa and WI, debt	Parliament, sent deputation	N			•
	Slave tax at Jamaica	Service offer	N			•
	Delay of postal service	PO	Y	•		
	Slave tax at Jamaica	BOT, sent deputation	Y			•
	Bounty on Greenland fishing	Parliament	N			•
	Smalls lighthouse and lighthouse taxes	Parliament delegation	N		•	
	Against letters patent on the content of porcelain	Parliament	?		•	
	Redress for plundering of shipwrecks	Parliament	N		•	
1775/6	Export of arms and ammunition to Africa	His majesty, sent deputation	Y			•
	Export of wheat etc to WI	Parliament	Y			•
	Lighthouse at Point of Ayr	Parliament	Y		•	

Date	Lobby topic	Target of lobby	Self-assessment of success (Y/N)	Field: local	Field: national	Field: international
1776	Need for new house of confinement and correction of vagrants	Liverpool mayor	Y	•		
1776/7	WI homeward convoys	Admiralty	Y?			•
	Naval protection on Africa coast	Admiralty	Y?			•
	Arming ships on Africa coast	His majesty	Y?			•
	Rendezvous of outward WI convoys at Cork not Spithead	Admiralty	Y			•
	Increased allowance of arms and ammunition for defence of ships	Privy Council	Y			•
	Supply of timber etc to Sugar Islands due to suspension of American trade	Parliament, sent deputation	N			•
	Lighthouse costs and Smalls	MP	?		•	
	Shipping of provisions from Ireland to WI	Privy Council	Y			•
1777	Convoy needs at Tortula	Admiralty	Y			•
	Unfair trading of Capt Johnson in Africa to be prosecuted and hostages recovered	Africa Committee London	?			•
	Convoy needs at Tortula	Admiralty	Y			•
	Protection from press of sailors at Liverpool	Admiralty	N	•		
	Maintenance of forts on Gold Coast	Africa Co	?			•
	Prevent encouragement of American privateering by WI	Ministers etc	?			•
	More cruisers to support non-convoy shipping to African and WI	Admiralty	?			•
	American privateering in WI (letter to Bristol qv)	Ministers etc	?	•		
	Extension of bond date on rum in warehouses	Treasury	N			•

Green, explicitly as chamber chair and secretary, with the Africa Company committee in London. Dobson and Green were asked to investigate and seek affidavits from witnesses about an incident in which a Captain Johnson was found guilty of leaving nine sailors at Badagry who had been taken prisoner on Cape Coast (Ghana). Green did this and also raised concerns from the father of one of the prisoners, Robert Grimshaw (who is a probable chamber member).[35] Additionally, Gill Slater, probably acting as a lead for the chamber, wrote twice in 1776/7 to the government's Committee for Trade seeking approval to overcome the embargo on export military stores during the American war. This was similar to other requests from Liverpool, Bristol and Glasgow; almost all were refused.[36] These cases indicate that the *Abstract* was a summary and was not complete for all chamber activities.

A major activity appears to have been a petition for conciliation with America, presented on 14 January 1775. This was developed in co-ordination with a national assembly in London of 300–400 merchants trading in America and over 200 West India merchants, who sought a "resistance … couched in decent and manly terms" to the government's action against the American colonies.[37] The petition was repeated in late 1775, where the Liverpool petitioners are included in the Lancashire County petition of "the gentlemen, traders and freeholders", concerned to re-establish peace with the American colonies. This was a crucial period in the chamber's development, and the heavy involvement of its members with petitioning marks a critical phase of tensions with the Liverpool Corporation, which petitioned in the opposite direction on both occasions, as discussed later. Hence, international trade could not be separated from national government policy and the attitudes of the local Corporation (which generally supported the government in opposition to the chamber).

National issues: lighthouses

Half of the national issues that were the focus of attention were concerned with the cost of lighthouses. This concern reflects a controversy of the time that the fees levied for lighthouses, by Trinity House or Municipal Corporation bodies that were responsible for them, were being directed into lavish dinners and entertainment for the 'brothers'

[35] Africa Company to John Dobson, chairman of chamber of commerce, 4 October 1776; to Samuel Green, secretary of the chamber of commerce, 21 and 31 December 1776, and 8 January, 1 and 8 February 1777; replying to letters from Green 25, 27 and 30 December 1776 and 4 January 1777: TNA T70/69.

[36] Journal of the Committee for Trade and Plantations, 18 July 1776, 3 June 1777; see also other entries for the other ports.

[37] Williamsons Advertiser 20 and 27 January 1775; see also Baines, 1852, pp 449–50; Bradley, 1986, p 22.

of the organisations, or benevolent schemes for their families.[38] The general validity of these concerns is reflected in the evidence collected by the Municipal Commission in the 1830s, which showed systematic diversion of resources in this way in many cases.[39] But in Liverpool there was the added point that shippers were already paying lighthouse fees, dock fees and town duties to the Corporation. The proposed lighthouse fee was a new tax where existing ones already provided sufficient revenue.

The Liverpool chamber was not opposed to the proposed lighthouses in principle, but was opposed to new fees: "the sums already exacted from shipping, under the pretence of contributions towards the support of lighthouses, are become so exorbitant, as justly to require public attention. That a very small part of the money, so exacted, is actually expended in the building and supporting of lighthouse and lights; ... the chief share being applied to the partial emolument of individuals."[40] The chamber resolved in 1775, repeated in 1776, "that every extension of lighthouses, under the management, and calculated only for the emolument of individuals, ought to be opposed by the public".[41] It was particularly enraged by the Smalls Light proposals.

The Smalls Lighthouse

The Smalls Light campaign shows the brevity of the *Abstract* compared with the chamber's actual activity. The initiative had been taken by John Phillips, who in 1773 proposed to Trinity House that he could improve the Skerries Light, and in 1774 applied to parliament for letters patent covering 50 years, to establish a light on the Smalls (off south Wales), financed by collecting duties from passing ships (but raised through the harbour authorities in the ports, including Liverpool and Bristol).[42] In February 1775 he presented a model of the proposed Smalls Light to Trinity House, but then went ahead and built it anyway without Trinity House agreement.[43] His expedition left Liverpool on 17 June 1775 and the light was completed on 1 September 1776.[44] Trinity House objected to Phillips petitioning parliament to erect the light himself, and they rejected overtures from Phillips offering a share of the money

[38] It should also be noted that the Liverpool ship-owners were already paying a fee to the Corporation for lights in the harbour approaches varying from a halfpenny to two pence per ton depending on length of voyage; Baines, 1852, p 431.

[39] Commission on Municipal Corporations (England and Wales), House of Commons Papers 1835-9.

[40] *Abstract*, 21 February 1775.

[41] Abstract, 21 February 1775, 12 October 1776.

[42] London Guildhall Archives: Trinity House Court Book, Ms. 30004/129; letters from John Phillips 5 June, 6 November 1773, 17 December 1774. Phillips had apparently had an interest in the Skerries and Smalls since 1765: Woods, 1949; Rees, 1949.

[43] Trinity House Court Book, Ms. 30004/129; letter from John Phillips 3 June 1775.

[44] Rees, 1949, pp 108-9.

raised.[45] However, Phillips obtained letters patent on 5 August 1774 and was levying dues by 1775. Trinity House initially took no action themselves, which was one aspect that annoyed the Liverpool chamber's merchants paying the new fees. Trinity House board even replied to the concerns of their collector of light duties at Bristol that, as they "have no concern in these lights, they cannot take or give instructions".[46]

It is less well known that Phillips was not acting alone, but in conjunction with Liverpool Corporation, through a group of the Corporation's trustees for the Smalls. Phillips had been employed by the Corporation as a dock master in 1770–3.[47] Initially the Corporation was opposed to Phillips' proposals for the Smalls. In February 1774 his petition was rejected as "impractical" … and "not proper or regular for them … to appear principals or otherwise". However, by March 1775 the Corporation had changed its view and supported Phillips' petition to parliament, passing it under the Corporation's seal.[48] They must have either constituted a new board of trustees for this purpose, or used the existing Corporation's Committee for Management of Lighthouses that in 1773 consisted of the mayor, bailiffs and eight others.[49] Trinity House certainly considered the Smalls trustees to be members of the Corporation working "under the mayor". We can identify two Corporation trustees who appeared before the Trinity House Board in 1778: William Crosbie (an alderman) and Thomas Golightly (who was town clerk). Though Phillips contended that there were a great number of other subscribers,[50] this must have meant the Corporation as an entity.

Phillips' initiative with the Corporation was another force energising the Liverpool chamber's active campaign. Here was another Corporation fee on top of other grievances that had led to the foundation of the chamber. The virulence of the grievance is again evidenced by Benjamin Heywood, who placed a series of cuttings of Phillips' letters to the local newspapers into his *Curious Papers* for the 1773–5 period. Phillips' extensive letter campaign defended his actions and ideas, mainly based on his need for money.[51]

Together with the Bristol Venturers,[52] the chamber petitioned parliament on 2 March 1775 against the Smalls proposal, opposing any

---

[45] Trinity House Board Minutes, Ms. 30010/15a; 7 January 1775, 10 February 1776.

[46] Trinity House Board Minutes, Ms. 30010/15a; 23 November 1776.

[47] One of John Parr's first actions as mayor in 1773 was for Phillips' salary to be made up to 100 guineas per year "for his diligent discharge as dock master on the North Dock": Corporation Council minutes, 18 October 1773.

[48] Corporation Council minutes, 15 February 1774; 1 March 1775. Rees, 1949, p 112 states that Phillips made over his interest to the Corporation, but the Council minutes make it clear they were involved from the start.

[49] Eg Corporation Council minutes, 4 August 1773.

[50] Trinity House Board Minutes, Ms. 30010/16; 3 January 1778; see also 21 June 1777.

[51] The main items are summarised in Woods, 1949.

[52] John Dobson, chair of Liverpool chamber, letter to SMV 10 April 1775; proceedings 24 April 1775, SMV/2/1/1/10.

perpetual tax on ships to support lighthouses on the grounds that[53] "a certain, perpetual, and almost a general tax (was inappropriate) for an uncertain, limited, and partial advantage". There was a vigorous co-ordination with Bristol, and use of their MPs Edmund Burke and Henry Cruger to lobby parliament. This had echoes of the tax resistance in the American colonies at the time. The fees paid by Liverpool merchants were differentiated by shipping destination. The highest fees were paid by Newfoundland and African ships at 12s 2d, and West Indian and American ships, at 18s 2d in 1772.[54] The recording of the Light fees, together with the dock duties, in Benjamin Heywood's *Papers* shows the irritation of the merchants of the time.

The chamber's campaign continued into 1778, though it is not recorded in the *Abstract*. Trinity House sought to make Phillips surrender his grant of letters patent, which they belatedly saw as an infringement of their rights, in return for granting him a lease. They negotiated with Phillips and the Liverpool Corporation trustees during 1777/8, finally reaching agreement on a new schedule of fees and a new Act of parliament to secure the position in February 1778. However, they agreed in June 1778 to assign Phillips a lease for 99 years.[55] This was opposed throughout by Liverpool chamber and the Bristol Venturers, as it had been in 1774–5.[56]

The views of the chamber were vindicated in 1826 when the Commons Select Committee on Lighthouses criticised Trinity House, which did "not possess the means of rendering an account of the amount collected by tonnage duty on shipping for any lights in the hands of individuals". For the Smalls lease to Phillips in 1778, the *net* income was judged excessive, reaching over £6,000 per year in 1818–22, and Trinity House was recommended to purchase the remaining lease.[57] They initially did nothing, net income continued to increase, but the remaining 41 years of the lease was finally purchased in 1836.[58]

The Point of Ayr Lighthouse

The Smalls conflict was in contrast to the attitude of the chamber over the lighthouse proposal at the Point of Ayr (near the mouth of the Dee

[53] *Abstract*, p 7.
[54] Notes in Heywood *Papers*.
[55] Trinity House Board Minutes, Ms. 30010/16; 8 and 26 March 1777; 29 November 1777; 3, 21, 27 and 31 January 1778; 4 February and 3 June 1778.
[56] SMV out-letter to Edmund Burke and Henry Cruger, Bristol MPs, 4 April 1777 to oppose Smalls Bill; SMV/2/4/1/1; Proceedings, SMV/2/1/1/10, quoting Liverpool chamber.
[57] House of Commons Accounts Reporting Lighthouses, 1826, XXI, pp 45–47; Select Committee on Lighthouses, House of Commons Papers, 1834; Bill for Vesting Lighthouses, 1835, III, p 333; 1836, IV, pp 319, 351.
[58] Rees, 1949, pp 114–6.

Estuary). In December 1775 it heard of this proposal by the City of Chester and opened immediate correspondence, reaching agreement: "such stipulations were agreed upon, as seemed calculated to prevent any inconveniences as to the Port of Liverpool". These negotiations with the managers of the Bill helped its passage in 1776.[59] This confirms the attitude of the chamber as not opposed to lighthouse costs per se, nor to Trinity House as managers, but to the specific costs and approach taken by Liverpool Corporation and the antics of Phillips regarding the Smalls.

Conversely, after the chamber gave its support for the Ayr light, the Corporation on this occasion initially opposed it, apparently because Chester was transgressing their cherished authority and control of charges over the port approaches. However, after their own negotiations with Chester and the managers of the Bill in Parliament, the Corporation came round to supporting the initiative.[60]

National campaigns: Corn Laws and patents

The other national issues lobbied over 1774–7 were varied. One was an early objection to the Corn Laws, where:[61] "A correspondence was entered into with Governor Pownall, upon the corn trade, which was productive of much important information upon the subject, and some new regulations, of great moment, were intended to be offered to the consideration of the legislature: but the unhappy disputes [American rebellion], which soon after broke out in a flame that still continues burning, have hitherto prevented the execution of these salutary schemes." This exchange relates to the 1773 Corn Law Act, which restructured Irish corn trade. Pownall, then MP and ex-governor of Massachusetts, was asked to frame the law.[62] Like Glasgow in 1777, Liverpool's activities reflect an early concern by chambers and the business community with the Corn Laws. It probably also reflects a particular aspect of John Dobson's chamber chairmanship, as he was a major corn dealer in Liverpool at the time. The Corn Laws emerged again for Liverpool in the 1790s, and were a running grievance of the chambers until the 1846 Corn Law abolition, led by the Manchester chamber.

Another national issue listed in the *Abstract* concerned resisting "a Bill then pending for enlarging the Terms of Letters Patent, for the sole use of certain materials for making porcelain. This restraint, it was

---

[59] *Abstract*, 7 December 1775, p 9.
[60] Corporation Council minutes, 3 January 1776; Committee of Trade minutes, 23 January, 6 May 1776.
[61] *Abstract*, 4 December, 1774, p 4.
[62] See eg Dirom, A. 1796, *An Inquiry into the Corn Laws and Corn trade of Great Britain with …Supplement*, William Creech, Edinburgh, p 134.

apprehended, would prevent such further improvements, as might be productive of most important advantages to trade".[63] This relates to the extension of a patent held by Richard Champion of Bristol, and a leading member of the Venturers. Liverpool's concern may interrelate with the interests of John Dobson who had been a partner in a pottery business, as well as pressures from Liverpool's agent for Josiah Wedgwood, Thomas Bentley, who was influential in Liverpool (though by then resident in London). Dobson was a joint investor with Wedgwood in the chinaware business of Reid & Co,[64] which was the first china manufacturing business in Liverpool, established in 1755 (closely followed by Richard Chaffers' china business, who was related to Edward Chaffers, another chamber member, established later in 1755). Other chamber members who had major pottery interests were Chaffers, the Lakes and the Rathbones. The single lobby on porcelain reflects this interest and was part of a major national campaign to resist Champion's patent.

At the same time a letter from Bristol seeking support for their petition to provide redress from plundering of shipwrecks, which was subsequently rejected by the House of Commons,[65] was also raised.

Local issues

The local issues which were the focus of lobbies concerned the postal service on two occasions; port facilities (seeking to increase "the number of land waiters, scale porters and scales for the use of this port");[66] and then two fields where national regulations were deemed locally to be overly restrictive – vulnerability to the pressgangs for the navy, and rules on rum bonds. The increase in land waiters etc reflects a similar concern to that of lighthouses: that the merchants were being asked to support ever more personnel and costs as a result of the Corporation's activities. In addition, appointments to these minor posts were frequently corrupt, through the patronage of the Corporation and/or government ministers and officers. However, the numbers of officials was less the concern than their costs and efficiency (through diligence and hours of attendance).[67] Thus this seemingly minor issue was in line with much of the chamber's general anger with Corporation levies and decisions.

The pressgangs were to become a concern again in the 1790s (see below), and were running concerns in all ports where the Navy

[63] *Abstract,* p 7–8, mid–1775.
[64] When Reid's went bankrupt in 1761, Dobson and Wedgwood were the chief creditors: Boney, 1957, particularly pp 127–9, 203–10. See also Meteyard, 1866.
[65] *Abstract,* p 8, mid–1775.
[66] *Abstract,* p 6, January 5, 1775.
[67] As shown in joint meetings with the Corporation's Committee of Trade: see later below.

desperately looked for manpower. The postal service was also to be a concern again in the 1780s. In 1774–5 the concern of the chamber was criticism with the departure time of the post on Fridays and Tuesdays. This was "the first public application made in the name of this society", "which was not acceded to".[68] However, a complaint about delayed mail in February 1775 was "immediately offered all the relief at that time in their power".[69] It appears that comments on postal service quality were met with better responses than requests for changes in its organisation.

The only lobby on a local body, the mayor, was for an improved house of confinement for vagrants. This attacked an issue of local notoriety. The old 'Tower or gaol' was leased by the Corporation and its purchase was being considered by the Corporation in 1774–5. Joseph Brooks (senior) produced a valuation on 2 August 1775 that would have allowed an agreement for purchase to be made, but the Corporation deferred the matter and did not finally agree to build a new gaol until 4 February 1783.[70] Here again was further frustration of the chamber members with the Corporation's activity or inactivity.

Effort and effect of voice

If we judge the seriousness of the concerns by the efforts made, and likely costs expended by the chamber, then five issues stand out. First, in January 1775, was the condition of American trade and debt, where William Meredith MP was used and three delegates from the chamber "attended several weeks in London".[71] Second, was the Jamaican slave duty, when in February 1775, "A numerous deputation from hence attended the Board of Trade …(where) the merchants of Liverpool had paid for this duty, in little more than six months £15,609 6s."[72] Third, was the March 1775 petition against the Smalls Bill, where there was considerable correspondence and co-ordination with the Bristol Venturers and their MPs, and two Liverpool delegates "attended and gave evidence in the House of Commons".[73] Fourth, was a 6 September 1775 deputation against the embargo on exporting of arms and ammunition. Fifth, were the "sundry petitions and memorials transmitted from hence to different Boards; and our representatives in parliament (who) exerted themselves" to procure a new supply of timber, stores, hoops

---

[68] *Abstract,* p 3, mid–1774.
[69] *Abstract,* p 5.
[70] Corporation Town Books: LRO:CLE/TRA/1/2/10.
[71] *Abstract, p 5.*
[72] *Abstract,* p 6; this was also a major concern of the Bristol Venturers: Out-letter to Edmund Burke, MP, 13 March 1775; SMV/2/4/1/1.
[73] *Abstract,* p 7.

etc for the Sugar Islands on 3 October 1776. These focuses again show the chief concerns to be for international trade, but also for domestic taxation, with the sub-theme being frustration with the Corporation.

The delegates who went to London to "attend" on behalf of the chamber were varied: on 26 January 1775, they were John Dobson (the chair), Samuel Haliday and John Walker. The "numerous delegation" on 14 February 1775 is not listed, but soon after, on 2 March, Edward Chaffers and Ambrose Lace appeared in the House, so it is likely that they acted as delegates on both occasions together with Dobson, Haliday and Walker from the previous attendance, and perhaps with others. On 6 September 1775 it was Thomas Case and Thomas Hodgson junior who attended in London. Whilst most of these can be identified as committee members of the chamber, there is no information that John Walker and Ambrose Lace were ever committee members (though Haliday joined the committee in 1780). This reinforces the interpretation that the chamber, although being a close-knit committee, at this time was also a broader body that could draw on the support of others (who must have been members) when required.

Was the lobbying successful? This is one of the most difficult questions to answer since frequently lobbying is recognised as more preparing the ground for changed policy rather than achieving immediate reversals. However, the *Abstract* for 1774–7, unusually, does give a self-assessment by its writer (presumably the secretary, Samuel Green) of effectiveness on most of the issues. This is summarised in Table 3. Whilst this may be an overly optimistic assessment, since it was written when new members and subscriptions were being sought, it has a ring of honesty probably born of the fact that its readers would know its veracity. Of the 35 issues, 15 (42.9%) were judged by the chamber as successful, a further three were probably successful, and three (marked with a query in Table 3) had some influence even if not entirely positive. Thus 65.7% had some positive outcome, as judged by the chamber's self-assessment. This is probably as good as, or better than, any modern lobby organisation. Most successful were lobbies on parliament over pending legislation, which were almost all successful. Least successful were some lobbies on the Admiralty to change convoy or protection measures, and matters beyond immediate government influence such as American debt and the Jamaican slave tax. However, for American debts, ultimate success was achieved in 1795, though long after the period covered by the *Abstract,* confirming that effective lobbying is often not evident by immediate returns but from persistence.

5
The chamber voice develops: 1777–87

The *Abstract* provides a nearly complete coverage of the lobbying activity of the chamber over its first three years. After that date we have only other more fragmentary sources. But these records generally evidence a continuation of the pattern established in the early years of the chamber.

Continuing international and national issues

In mid–1777 John Dobson, still chamber chair, was corresponding frequently with Lord Germain to draw attention to, and seeking compensation for, privateering by the French and Americans on the Guinea Coast, Martinique, St Lucia and around Ireland.[74] Also, as noted above, in late 1777 and through 1778 the major lobby on the Smalls Bill continued, opposed by the Corporation, with Dobson, Slater and Staniforth all involved. It is clear from the Bristol papers that Liverpool chamber was the leading player in opposition to this Bill (opposing the Corporation's trustees), with Bristol in support.[75]

---

[74] Letters 23 May and 20 June 1777, to Lord Germain, copied to Pitt (TNA: SP 78/302, f. 335, 419; SP 78/303 f. 105, 107 114).
[75] Letters from Dobson and Slater 16 February 1778, and Staniforth 6 March 1778, referred to in SMV out-letters of support to Slater 26 February and 20 April, 1778; to Staniforth 14 March 1778, SMV/2/4/1/1; Proceedings SMV/2/1/1/10.

In late 1778 concern also continued with how captured prizes were dealt with.[76] Fresh concerns with the Africa Company in London led to further exchanges with Bristol in April 1779, where Liverpool and Bristol as the two outports with their own freeman of the Africa Company joined to resist the London interest. Liverpool chamber saw this as an attack on their trade and were "much alarmed at the advantages the advocates for monopoly were likely to receive from the abuse of the present establishment" and were "working with the different members [MPs] in this and the neighbouring counties". This crossed with a letter from Bristol to the Liverpool chamber expressing the same concerns.[77] However, the chamber was in continued exchange with the Africa Company on other matters, the president of the chamber (unnamed) being informed in 1783 about the Committee's actions on north American rum.[78] In 1781 the Committee of Merchants of Liverpool (probably the chamber) presented a petition to parliament criticising the conduct of British Naval Commanders in the American War at St Eustatia.[79]

But one of the most important trading issues of this period was over proposals for open trade with Ireland and the West Indies. This had begun to be an issue under North's government in 1778, when the Corporation had sought to oppose developments and marshalled other towns to follow suit.[80] But the issue re-emerged once the American war was ended in 1783. In 1784 John Tarleton senior, writing to Pitt on behalf of "the chamber of commerce in this place", suggested that the planters were preparing a petition in favour of direct intercourse between the West Indies and America. Tarleton noted that "the chamber of commerce in this place was earnestly requested by the London Committee" (the West India Committee, and the London Committee of Merchants Trading in America) to produce a counter-petition if Pitt advised them to do so. It is unclear whether the proposed opposition was the chamber's view or Tarleton's own. Tarleton was certainly opposed to erosion of the Navigation Laws which would "sacrifice the most necessary restrictions, end our whole colonial and commercial system; the work of ages". The offer by Tarleton is interesting since it shows him trying to ingratiate himself with the new prime minister, Pitt,

---

[76] SMV letter to Liverpool chamber re: captured prizes; out-letters, SMV/2/4/1/1, 30 December 1778.
[77] Gill Slater to, 12 April 1779; SMV/2/4/2/22 (18); SMV out-letters, SMV/2/4/1/1, 8 April 1779; Slater and draws attention to votes in the Commons in favour of the Africa Company inviting them to join in opposition; Proceedings 8 April 1779, SMV/2/1/10.
[78] Africa Committee to president of Liverpool chamber of commerce, 16 September 1783; TNA T70/69.
[79] 14 May 1781; presented by Burke, MP for Bristol, not by the MPs for Liverpool, Gascoyne and Rawlinson: *London Magazine* or *Gentleman's Monthly Intelligencer*, L, 1781, p 381; also supported by Committee of Trade 3 March 1781.
[80] Corporation minutes; Committee of Trade minutes 28 March, 6, 15 and 18 April, 2 November, 24 December 1778; 22 February, 15 March 1779.

perhaps on behalf of his son's political ambitions (the chamber member) to work *with* the government, jointly to stem adverse legislation by orchestrating local action. Tarleton sought Pitt's advice, "happy to coincide with his Lordship [Pitt], to avert an evil of such magnitude ... I beg to hear from you ... and to receive from you a general ground of opposition to the above measures if you think my idea of obtaining a protest here will have any effect with government or the House".[81] This may show the Liverpool chamber to be generally in opposition to the colonial planters, but it may be a distortion by Tarleton (as enlarged further below).

Customs House fees and practices

In early 1782 the chamber was concerned about the costs of the Customs service and approached Bristol for support for information and a lobby. The costs of Customs at Liverpool had grown significantly. Whilst in 1760–70 it had remained at just over £100,000, by 1780 it had grown to £175,000, and had reached £350,000 by 1790. This was of course partly as a result of the growing trade of the port.[82] But it was also seen as a result of new Customs fees, an over-expanded business that was nevertheless providing a poor service, and unauthorised perks for the Customs controller.

In 1782 the chamber had been "collecting an account of innovations and useless expenses of our Custom House".[83] They complained that Isle of Man bonds were being used as a general impost, "when now that the Isle was under the Crown", these were no longer required. In the same letter, Gill Slater also informed Bristol that a general petition was being got up seeking reinforcements to protect British interests in the West Indies. Bristol agreed to support both.[84]

The Customs service issue rumbled on. Between December 1781 and March 1782 the chamber held 11 joint meetings with the Corporation's committee of trade, with William Gregson (for the Corporation) and Gill Slater (for the chamber) as joint chairs. The report of these meetings covers 13, 20 and 27 December 1781, 23 and 25 February, and 4, 11, 15, 16 and 20 March 1782. The final meeting on 25 March 1782 produced a new set of proposed rules and regulations which specified the hours when Customs officers should be in attendance, allowed the consolidation of goods from one business transaction into a single Customs entry (overcoming the abuse that officers were levying on individual items to benefit their pockets), and set fees for every

[81] Letter from John Tarleton, 23 June 1784; TNA: PRO 30/8/182 f. 19, 26–7.
[82] LRO 942 HOL/19, p 73.
[83] Letter from Slater, 4 January 1782, SMV/2/4/2/24 (1).
[84] SMV out-letter, 21 January 1782 to Henry Cruger MP supporting Liverpool's request, SMV/2/4/1/1.

Customs, storekeeper and other report, debenture, bond and other transaction in 43 categories.[85]

This produced some accommodation with the Customs. But it was not until 1785, when a new local Controller of Customs was appointed (Arthur Onslow), that reforms got fully underway. Another further joint effort was mounted, and the chamber and the committee of trade received a letter from Onslow in answer to their concerns. Onslow offered to employ more clerks, to lengthen the hours, and improve the speed with which his office could operate, and also suggested a new schedule of charges, the most controversial element of which was the payment of one-eighth percent with debentures on bills in lieu of cash. We do not know the chamber's response. The Corporation's committee of trade thanked Onslow for improving the manning of the offices, but unanimously rejected the proposed method of payment.[86]

Other activities

Another joint effort between the chamber and the Corporation's committee of trade was mounted in July 1782 over the process of quarantine of ships. Gill Slater (chamber chair) and John Brown (committee chair) wrote to the Collector and Controller of Customs requesting that the location for quarantine be shifted to the Hilbre Islands (between the Mersey and Dee) or the Bromborough Pool. These were more sheltered and larger than the Twyndee Point, which was too shallow, whilst the roadstead at Hoylake was too small.[87]

Further joint action between the chamber and the committee of trade was undertaken in August 1782, to petition for a new Act for better regulation of pilots and ferries at Liverpool.[88] There is no further detail on this, but it would appear that there was unhappiness with availability, soundness and costs of the pilots and ferries. These three actions jointly with the Corporation committee of trade over 1781–5 show that some of the enmities that had existed in 1774–5 had been overcome, and the chamber was seeking to try to persuade the Corporation to use its powers to overcome some regulatory failures.

In this period the chamber's secretary, Samuel Green, also contacted the Africa Committee in London in 1786 seeking stronger support from the Navy for shipping in Africa. The town clerk had also written, and support was being sought from Bamber Gascoyne MP, with the Africa Committee used as further support.[89]

---

[85] Corporation Committee of Trade, minutes 25 March 1782; LRO 352 MIN/COM I 2/1.

[86] Corporation Committee of Trade, minutes 27 July 1787, containing letter from Arthur Onslow and resolution in reply; LRO 352 MIN/COM I 2/1.

[87] Corporation Committee of Trade, minutes 8 July 1782; LRO 352 MIN/COM I 2/1.

[88] Corporation Committee of Trade, minutes 30 August 1782; LRO 352 MIN/COM I 2/1.

The Post Office

In late 1782 the concern of the chamber with the postal service continued. Gill Slater, writing as the chamber chair, complained about the delays and quality of deliveries by the Post Office, eg on "Thursdays letters [are] not delivered till 8 in the evening".[90] Receiving no action from the Post Office itself, this was followed up by a memorandum of the Merchants of Liverpool to the Prime Minister, Pitt, delivered by the Liverpool MP, Bamber Gasgoyne.[91] This stated that "Complaints against the mode of management ... had long been great and frequent." The chamber "supported the methods of service delivery instituted by John Palmer at Bath".

Palmer's plan was for the first mail coach service (replacing post boys on horseback). It began on 2 August 1784 as an experiment from Bath and Bristol to London, with the sanction of Pitt. Palmer had tried to establish a country-wide mail coach service through a *Plan* he promulgated in 1782. This had been supported by the Shelburne–Rockingham government, which had included Pitt. The Liverpool chamber must have heard of this *Plan*, the letter from Slater to the General Post Office giving strong support to the proposals. However, the Post Office was very resistant to change, raising "three volumes of objections" by July 1783 that declared it "absolutely impractical". With a change in government to Fox and North the plan was postponed, but was taken up again in December 1783 when Pitt became prime minister; the Post Office lodged another volume of objections, but Pitt overrode them to allow the trial. The trial was highly successful, and Pitt, against further trenchant resistance from the GPO, allowed its extension. By mid-1785 mail coaches covered all the main centres in England, including Liverpool, and later Scotland.[92] In 1786 Palmer was appointed surveyor and comptroller general of the GPO, but conflicts with the conservative forces within continued and his resignation was forced in 1792.

For Liverpool the new mail coach service to London began on 5 July 1785, taking 35 hours. At the end of 1786 the chamber secretary wrote to Gascoyne and Palmer expressing gratitude for their help in reform

---

[89] Africa Company reply of 8 September to letters from Samuel Green, 2 September, and John Colquitt 28 August 1786; TNA T70/145.

[90] Letter from Gill Slater, President of Liverpool chamber of commerce, to Anthony Todd Esq., GPO, 12 December 1782: LRO MD/1.

[91] Memorandum, 17 August 1784; LRO MD/2.

[92] John Palmer, *Plan for the reform and improvement of the General Post Office*, 1782; see also *Papers relative to the agreement made by the government with Mr Palmer for the reform and improvement of the Posts*, London, 1797; also Vale, 1967, pp 10–38.

and asking that their gratitude be "presented to the minister".[93] The chamber's involvement in Palmer's campaign represents the first foray of UK chambers into this field, but the mails were to be a continuous source of grievance by chambers into the 20th century, with many campaigns against the inefficiencies and costs of the GPO.[94]

The postal service saga showed an early phase of Liverpool's willingness to oppose the London merchants' interests. These were often aligned with Liverpool on questions of trade, but on internal matters (except over John Wilkes' campaign for electoral reform) London often aligned with conservatives to resist change. Some of the leading London merchants were certainly willing to be used to support the resistance of the GPO to Palmer's *Plan*. They called a meeting in February 1786 to oppose the change of closing time of the GPO, which had been brought forward to 7.00 pm to meet the time of departure of the mail coaches at 8.00 pm, and other changes that they believed inconvenienced them. They were also influenced by a vociferous lobby from GPO appointees around the country who might lose their jobs. Pitt ignored these protests. But when Palmer later made himself vulnerable, the London merchants were again used by the GPO, and at a meeting on 15 February 1792 they supported Palmer's removal from office, which occurred later in the year.[95] This is an important early indication of the differentiation of the regional and Atlantic trading interests of Liverpool from those of some other areas, and the backing by chambers of general processes of reform.

Relations with other chambers

In 1779 Gill Slater, chair of the chamber, had sent a Manchester chamber petition to the Bristol Venturers to elicit their support for an Act for the importation of cotton wool in neutral shipping duty-free during the present war. The Venturers sent this to their West India merchants, who could not agree, and also to the Bristol MPs seeking their advice.[96] In the end they made no reply. This is an important early indication of a division of emphasis emerging between the manufacturing centres, such as Manchester, and the ports engaged in the Atlantic trade, where Bristol was either not concerned, or too divided to take a view.

[93] Letter from Samuel Green, Secretary of the Liverpool chamber of commerce to Bamber Gascoyne MP and John Palmer Esq, 31 December 1786; LRO MD/3.
[94] See Bennett, 2011, Chapter 10; Ilersic and Liddle, 1960, pp 123–8.
[95] The mail coach story surrounding Palmer is complex and full of political intrigue and personalities that cannot be covered here: see Vale, 1967.
[96] Slater letter 6 December 1779; SMV 2/1/1/10; out-letter to Gill Slater president of Liverpool chamber, 7 December 1779; SMV/2/4/1/1.

From 1783 a second phase of chamber establishment had occurred, and Liverpool was in contact with the new Glasgow chamber in particular. Liverpool responded to Glasgow chamber's requests in 1783 to support a memorial from the manufacturers of iron, and also to join in a memorial on the tobacco and sugar trades.[97] Gill Slater offered the support of the chamber after consulting the committee at its next regular meeting in April 1783. He was "directed to enquire what further steps you [Glasgow] intend taking in regard to a drawback upon foreign iron wrought up here for export into nails etc".

Slater's letter follows an earlier acknowledgement to Glasgow from Samuel Green of 23 March, sent in Slater's absence. In fact both Green's and Slater's letters are written in Green's hand, and in both letters the main space is devoted to sugar and tobacco, not iron. The end of the war with America and France offered opportunities for re-establishing and regularising these trades. Green wrote: "Amidst the many important articles relative to commerce which have for some time engaged the attention of this society, the utility of restoring to Britain some share in the export of tobacco has claimed much attention. The high duty, required by the laws now in force, to be paid down before landing, must confine our import to the small quantity necessary for home consumption only; and effectually exclude us from a chance of the least share in supporting other European markets." Green suggested "joint efforts towards the arrangements wanted" by "every considerable seaport in the Kingdom". Slater's letter repeated the request regarding tobacco, that Liverpool chamber "much wishes to join the other principal places of importation in pursuing this object with spirit". However, for "Sugar, being the production of another country, it may perhaps be better not to include in the same application, particularly at this time, when the plantation and mercantile interests in London, Bristol etc. have solicited us to join them in an application to parliament, for a reduction in duties on sugar and rum. We very readily closed with the proposal, and only wait their appointing a time for throwing in the petitions."[98]

In fact, the Bristol Venturers were not supportive of the efforts by Liverpool and Glasgow, sending a very off-putting reply to Glasgow's secretary: "Upon due consideration it appears to them on the first mentioned memorial [on iron], the drawback proposed would be impractical in most instances, and impolitic in all; and as to the second

---

[97] A memorial was a formally considered position paper with a request for action. Glasgow chamber letters to Liverpool, Bristol and manufacturing towns of England, referred to in minutes 7 March 1783; TD 76/1; letters from Glasgow of 15 and 25 March to Liverpool referred to in reply by Gill Slater to Gilbert Hamilton secretary of Glasgow chamber, 12 April 1783; TD 1670/4/15.

[98] Samuel Green, secretary Liverpool chamber of commerce to Gilbert Hamilton, 23 March 1783; Gill Slater to Hamilton, 12 April 1783; TD 1670/4/15.

memorial [on tobacco and sugar], it does not appear that the duties deposited lie inappropriated, and if so, the argument to be built on the fact cannot be supported, but it will be further enquired into."[99] As in 1779, when Liverpool approached Bristol on behalf of the Manchester chamber, the Venturers were not very interested in becoming engaged in the problems of the manufacturers.

These records show that Liverpool chamber was continuing to liaise with other areas. The co-operation with the newly-founded Glasgow chamber over problems in the tobacco and sugar trades moved on to concerns about new taxes from Pitt's government, formed in 1782.[100] By March 1783, the co-operation between the main cities was expanding to include "other manufacturing towns of England" in a more general concern about taxation and Pitt's trade propositions with Ireland.[101] These exchanges were part of the build-up to a concerted action by a wide range of business groups across Britain and Ireland, including all the early chambers, to lobby Pitt against a fustian tax on dyed stuffs and cotton goods, and then on proposals to introduce a more open trade between England and Ireland. The conjunction of interests on these various government proposals led to a large number of provincial business representatives being together in London in early 1785. This allowed a high level of interchange, which led to the formation of a General Chamber of Manufacturers.

The period of the General Chamber of Manufacturers 1785–7

A General Chamber of Manufacturers was formed in 1785 as a national representative body. It survived until it collapsed in discord in 1787. This was a body that appointed a secretary in London to act as a co-ordinator of various 'provincial chambers' and delegates. It had some outstanding success against the younger Pitt's early government on taxation and reform of trade with Ireland.

This is not the place to review the history of the General Chamber. What is critical here is to recognise how *some* major 'provincial' mainly manufacturing interests were becoming aligned and represented by a single 'national' body. However, for different areas the outcomes were different. For Glasgow and Dublin, each with their own chamber of commerce, both founded in 1783, and for Liverpool, there was an explicit strategy of working with the General Chamber, but also lobbying

---

[99] Samuel Worrall, secretary of SMV, to Gilbert Hamilton, 12 April 1783; TD 1670/4/15.
[100] Glasgow Chamber, minutes 18 February 1783, mention co-operation with Liverpool chamber.
[101] Glasgow Chamber, minutes 3 March 1783.

independently of it.[102] They never accepted the General Chamber as *the* national voice, but saw it merely as a co-ordinator of some of the local interests. However, for the North Staffordshire potteries, Birmingham and Manchester, where their local chamber of commerce leaders (respectively, Josiah Wedgwood, Samuel Garbett and Thomas Walker) became also the leading national figures (joint vice-presidents) of the General Chamber, there were problems of separating local and national identity.

As far as can be ascertained, the Liverpool chamber was not a member of the General Chamber and it acted like Glasgow, working at arm's length of it through its MP.[103] The General Chamber was initiated in order to attack two proposals: a tax on fustians, which particularly angered Manchester; and a Bill for open trade with Ireland. The Liverpool chamber was not concerned about fustians, but on the Irish proposals it appears to have been aligned with the general body of Liverpool merchants, which drew up the *first* petition presented to parliament. The petition was presented by government supporter Bamber Gasgoyne MP on 3 March 1785.[104] It was phrased in temperate terms, supporting Pitt's own concept of trade benefits from more open trade, but drew attention to the large and open coast of Ireland which could be used as a means for smuggling, as well as legal importation from the plantations, which could then be clandestinely introduced to England. It concluded by "praying, that the privilege of supplying her own markets with the produce of her own colonies may be preserved inviolate to this kingdom, and that every farther extension of trade between Great Britain and Ireland may be established upon such equitable principles, as will redound equally to the mutual benefit of both countries".[105] This is quite different in emphasis from the Corporation's committee of trade, which opposed open trade with Ireland and the West Indies in 1778–9. The chamber and general merchant community was thus more supportive than the Corporation.

The Liverpool and Glasgow lobbies were also distinctive in not challenging established procedures; they worked with traditional power-brokers and MPs: what Glasgow termed "temperate opposition".[106] The General Chamber's approach, through Walker, was deliberately populist and worked with the Whig opposition. Its petition in Manchester, variously claimed to have 40,000 or 50,000 signatures,

---

[102] See Bennett, 2011, Chapter 9; Glasgow minutes, Report of Delegates, June 1785; TD 76/1 pp 136–145; for Dublin see Cullen, 1983.
[103] Glasgow Chamber, minutes, Report of Delegates, June 1785, op. cit.
[104] The petition was from "the gentlemen, merchants and others, inhabitants of Liverpool".
[105] Parliamentary History, 1785, p 348.
[106] Glasgow Chamber, minutes, Report of Delegates, June 1785, op. cit.

was more of a mass protest, like those supporting John Wilkes over election reform. This populism was a direct challenge to authority, and resulted in the General Chamber being perceived to be a direct political tool of the opposition. This led to internal dissent between General Chamber members for and against the government, which led to disputes over the lobby on the subsequent Eden Treaty with France. These disputes resulted in collapse of the General Chamber in 1787. The significance of these developments is to show that Liverpool and Glasgow were developing a different approach to chamber representations than that of the 'new manufacturers' in the General Chamber. Liverpool and Glasgow chambers were part of a different voice for the Atlantic trading interests, and generally more open trade. They were similarly differentiated from London on some issues, as the reforms of the mail service had demonstrated.

Other concerns 1777–87

Contemporaneous with these developments, it is possible that Henry Wilckens became chair of the chamber in 1786–7, because of the number of his letters, not on matters directly affecting his business, sent to Lord Hawkesbury the President of the Committee on Trade. Wilckens had no previous political activity of this kind. However, he at no time mentions the chamber, referring instead to issues that "come to my attention". Although he was primarily a salt manufacturer and trader, in 1786–7 he wrote on: the proposed duty on fir balk staves; the treaty with France and the ordinances of the port of Dunkirk that prevented the export of corn in other than French vessels; and the need to codify insurance laws, where Britain was "most behind other countries: and suffered from fickle, indeterminate and even frequently quite opposite law decisions, … which has given a plentiful harvest to pettifoggers." At the same time he also wrote on matters closer to his own business: the need to rectify Irish "trifling duties" on imported fish as unfair in comparison to Greenland fishery imports into Britain; and the exports of salt and its smuggling from Ireland to Wales and south-west England, which also added to impediments on fisheries.[107]

---

[107] Henry Wilckens letters to Lord Hawkesbury: 8 Dec 1786, 7 Jan 1787, 19 March 1787: BL Add MS 38221 f.11, f.98–9, f.292–3; Hawkesbury's reply on navigation laws at Dunkirk was that he did not want any notice drawn to them in order not to make the French more aware of Britain's navigation laws, but he asks Wilckens for more information on the laws of insurance: BL Add MS 38309, f. 146.

6
The slave trade abolition debate 1787/8

A critical period for the chamber must have been the emergence of the slave trade abolition movement in 1787. It has been stated that no member of the Corporation or significant ship-owners in Liverpool in this period could have been outside the trade (except Wallace who was opposed on religious grounds),[108] and many picked up slave cargoes as a result of privateering even if this was not one of their main concerns.[109] As shown later, the chamber had a large membership from slave traders, as to be expected in Liverpool, but it also had many not involved in the trade, and a number definitely in favour of abolition (notably William Wallace, who became a founding member of the abolition society, and Joseph Rathbone as a Quaker).[110] Previously insufficiently recognised is the support for abolition from Edgar Corrie, in some more limited form even from Thomas Hodgson junior (members of the chamber), and possibly even from Richard Watt senior (uncle of chamber member Richard, and a factor for sale of slaves at Jamaica), even though these were all involved in the trade. Thus the chamber had members both for and against abolition.

---

[108] See Touzeau, 1910; Sanderson, 1977; Drescher 1986; Longmore 2007.
[109] See Williams, 1897, p 613–4; see also Hyde, et al, 1951.
[110] Only one African shipping merchant was completely outside this trade, William Wallace, a chamber member, reputedly as a result of his Catholic convictions. He was a founding member of the Abolition Society in Liverpool: Brooke, 1853; Williams, 1897; Drescher 1986; Howman, 2007; Longmore, 2007.

Support for abolition

The dilemma for the supporters of abolition is clear from Edgar Corrie, who wrote to Hawkesbury in February 1788 offering his support for abolition and providing an anonymous memorandum arguing the commercial case. Both were sent in secret.[111] Corrie states: "I am a merchant of Liverpool, and it might be attended with irreparable prejudice to some branches of the business in which I am engaged, that I stood forth with any opinion that could favour the abolition of the slave trade." Therefore he "begs that this private letter may not be communicated to any person unless to Mr Pitt" and that his accompanying memorandum (which is signed MJ) be not transmitted to any "but the transcribing clerk, and that any communication of that letter be made from a transcribed copy", and that "my name must remain an invisible secret, not to be communicated to Mr Wilberforce or to the world".

Corrie's extraordinary letter shows the pressures on individuals from the interlocked business networks in Liverpool. It shows that there can be strong negatives arising from networks. As observed by Sanderson,[112] the Liverpool abolitionists "preferred to work under cover, not seeking the kind of publicity that would bring them to the notice of the African traders of their home town". Corrie's letters also demonstrate that there were leading local merchants sympathetic to abolition and very critical of the stand taken by the Corporation and many of their colleagues. Corrie states that: "It must be the desire of the government to prove the best information on this subject and if possible reverse the prejudices of the Town of Liverpool by unquestionable evidence." His memorandum seeks to provide that evidence, and he refers to Thomas Hodgson junior and Richard Watt as sharing his views.

Corrie's memorandum is long and need not detain us here.[113] What is significant is the evidence it offers of what must have been a divided chamber membership. It is now clear that among the chamber's committee, as well as Corrie, there were Wallace and Rathbone, and possibly Thomas Hodgson junior and Richard Watt junior who were supporters of abolition.

---

[111] Edgar Corrie to Hawkesbury 24 Feb 1788; and "memorandum by M.J."; BL Add MS 38416, f.35–6, 37–44; see also Donnan, 1931, p 656.

[112] Sanderson, 1989, p 197; Howman, 2007.

[113] Essentially he argues that there had been no commercial benefit from Britain's supremacy in the slave trade; that the need for new supplies of slaves largely derived from the abuse of the existing slaves by the planters; that Jamaica in particular was overstocked; the negro population should be allowed to develop families and women absolved from work; and that the slave trade had diverted Liverpool merchants from other lucrative trades, particularly developing direct reverse trade with Africa, and the development of farming in Africa.

Resistance to abolition

At the same time as Corrie's letter and the initiatives by Wallace and others, many of the other chamber members and committee were joining with the Corporation in vigorously opposing abolition. For example, contemporary with Corrie's letter, Henry Wilckens, probably the chamber president at the time, although "never directly or indirectly involved" in the slave trade, wrote to Hawkesbury arguing that the trade should not be wholly abolished but policy focused on removing abuses;[114] whilst John Tarleton wrote focusing on the difficulties of removing abuses if legislation is focused on restricting the trade to larger ships (as advocated in the parliamentary Bill of William Dolben).[115] John Tarleton was a leading member of the Corporation's delegation to parliament in 1788, but was the only delegate who was a known or probable member of the chamber.[116]

Managing divisions

Thus the chamber's membership was deeply divided. Although we have no formal records, the Hawkesbury and other papers evidence the division and this must explain why there is no record of the chamber playing any role as a voice for or against abolition. None of the parliamentary papers and debates on the slave trade mentions the chamber, and there are no correspondence items that have been found: it chose to sit in the background. Similarly, in correspondence on the slave trade from the Bristol Venturers, which vigorously campaigned against abolition, there is no record of any reply or active involvement from the chamber; indeed John Tarleton asked for his *personal* expenses in opposition to the Bill to be covered by the Venturers, with no reference to the chamber.[117] It is likely that Liverpool chamber decided, like Glasgow chamber on the same slave trade issue in 1788, that "because members of the chamber held different views", it was "not expedient that the directors of the chamber should take any decisive resolutions", but instead should leave developments to the "wisdom of parliament".[118]

---

[114] Henry Wilckens letters to Hawkesbury 5 and 15 March 1788; BL Add MS 38416 f.51–2, 53–5. Wilckens also published many of his letters as a public attack on Dolben's Bill: *Letters concerning the slave trade and with respect to its intended abolition by a merchant to a friend*; Liverpool Athenaeum, Misc. papers 49.

[115] John Tarleton letters to Hawkesbury 25 May and 9 and 26 June 1788; BL Add MS 38416, f.90–2, 103–6, 133.

[116] The other members of the delegation were Robert Norris, James Penny (called Parry by Thorne), John Matthews and Archibald Dalzell; see Corporation minutes and RG Thorne, 1986, *History of Parliament*; also Picton 1886, pp 215–6; Sanderson, 1972.

[117] SMV out-letters 31 July 1789 to Tarleton, and 18 March 1789 to the Liverpool chamber, on the Slave Bill; SMV/2/4/1/2. His request was declined!

[118] Glasgow chamber minutes, 14 Oct 1788; TD 76/1.

Samuel Green's ambiguous role

That the chamber sat in the background is further evidenced by the changed role of its secretary, Samuel Green. He played an active role in co-ordinating information from the merchants and ship-builders on the probable effects of the shipping tonnage limitation proposed by Dolben. He also co-ordinated all the correspondence and wrote most of the material for the Liverpool campaign against abolition. Some of his calculations on the scale of shipping and cargoes involved in the slave trade, and his calculations of financial losses and jobs dependent on the trade remain some of the most valuable sources for this period. He calculated that in 1790 £1.074m of capital was devoted to the slave trade and that at least 5,000 jobs depended on it. Jobs were threatened on 135 ships, estimated to cover 24,557 tons, with 3,814 sailors whose wages of £320,000 would disappear. Green also estimated a threat to over 1,000 ancillary jobs in ship-building and maintenance etc.[119]

Green was active enough against abolition for a pension of £300 and expenses to be awarded to him by the Corporation, which after his death was converted to an annuity for his widow, in recognition of his work in fighting abolition. This was "for his five years attendance as secretary to the African delegates and Liverpool African Committee, and also £42 during the preceding two years together with £25 of expenses".[120] The Corporation minutes on the grant to Green are revealing. They report that a committee chaired by George Case had considered the cases for Green, as well as Robert Norris and James Penny, delegates from the Corporation against the slave trade abolition. The Corporation found it straightforward to conclude that Norris and Penny should be awarded remuneration by the Corporation. But for Green the sympathy for supporting him, clearly pressed by the mayor, Clayton Tarleton, had to be based on a long-winded argument of how he had been employed by the Corporation. They had to make reference to actions "sometimes under the directions of the chief magistrates, sometimes at the instance of the committee on trade and sometimes of the members of the Council under an implied faith of compensation being made". … "and that for the past seven years of such service he has not received any manner of recompense". The case for Corporation support was concluded to rest on him having appeared "to have been employed as secretary and agent of the London delegates of the Liverpool African Committee as well as general letter writer to all the

---

[119] 'Calculations by Samuel Green', reported in LRO Holt Gregson papers 942 HOL/10, pp 367–375.
[120] Memorandum for council meeting of 2 February 1793, added to margin of Corporation minutes of 5 December 1792, signed by Clayton Tarleton mayor; see also Williams, 1897, pp 613–4, n.97.

different members of parliament and other persons with whom it was necessary to keep up a correspondence upon the African proceedings for the space of nearly five years";[121] ie over 1785–92.

These minutes show Green to have been at the centre of all the lobby activities in Liverpool of this period, not only the chamber. But for the slave trade opposition he was acting independently of the chamber. This is further confirmed by his letters on the slave trade all using the address of the Liverpool African Committee Room.[122] He wrote as secretary of that committee. His use of the committee address seems to have been ad hoc during the anti-abolition campaign.[123] He also acted as secretary of the Corporation's committee of trade for a short period during their campaign against abolition, their minutes showing his distinctive handwriting as the clerk for the period 24 July–3 August 1789. There is no doubt therefore that Green was compromised, and could not use his position as chamber secretary on the slave trade issue, although other correspondence over the same period on other issues shows that he remained also as the chamber secretary over this time.

[121] Common Council, minutes of 5 December 1792.

[122] Eg Samuel Green to Hawkesbury, 21 and 30 May 1788; BL Add MS 38416, f. 93, 96.

[123] See Liverpool Africa Committee minutes LRO 352 MD 1. Unfortunately a letter from Green to the SMV on about 11–26 February 1788 is missing from the Venturers archive and is only recorded in the index, with no listing of address; its catalogue reference is SMV/2/4/2/29 (10).

7
Other chamber business 1787–92

Despite the divisions over slave trade abolition which prevented the chamber taking a view, it appears that it continued very actively lobbying on other matters. In September 1787 Bristol approached the chamber over a House of Lords proposal to abolish fees at Customs houses, which followed up the earlier concerns of the chamber.[124] In April 1788 Samuel Green wrote as chamber secretary to Lord Penryn lobbying against the Bill intended to encourage whale fishing in the southern hemisphere. The chamber objected to the bounty to be paid to foreigners to do this, and argued that previous foreign expeditions had brought in no whales whilst there were no difficulties in northern waters.[125]

In the period of negotiating the treaty with France in 1785–7, Bristol and Liverpool were in contact over the terms, independently of the General Chamber.[126] Henry Wilckens, probably again chamber president in 1789–90, was recipient of letters from Lord Hawkesbury regarding United Italy in 1789, and in 1790 he was cautioning Wilckens that for

[124] SMV out-letter to Liverpool chamber, 8 September 1787; SMV/2/1/2/3.
[125] Samuel Green, secretary of the chamber to Lord Penryn, 21 April 1788; BL Add MS 38223 f.39–40.
[126] Letter from Liverpool deputies to SMV regarding the French trade treaty, 24 July, 1787; SMV/2/4/1/2.

Liverpool now is not the right time for a petition on American trade: the Committee on Trade "have different sentiments from the merchants of Liverpool".[127] In early 1790 Wilckens, referring to "those gentlemen at whose requests I have taken the freedom to write this letter", agitated about the Average Tonnage and Duty Bill in America, where Liverpool "gentlemen … become every day now anxious", and "the trade desire" equalisation of all duties with America.[128]

In 1790–1 Green wrote four further letters to the government Committee on Trade, explicitly as the chamber secretary, raising questions about the export quotas on grain from Liverpool to the West Indies, whether unfilled monthly quotas could be carried forward to the next month, and asking for leave for John Brown of Liverpool to export barley and beans to Gibraltar.[129] The Committee generally agreed to these requests (except Brown's request on Gibraltar) in line with similar requests from Bristol and Glasgow that had similar quota demands.

In 1790–1 and 1791–2 Edgar Corrie was probably chamber chair as he sent a stream of letters to Hawkesbury: on the need for better records of ships, tonnage and duties at Liverpool; a lengthy statement on cotton consumption 1789–92 and estimates for 1791–92.[130] However, the greatest weight of his correspondence over 1790–2 relates to the Corn Laws. The Corn Law letters concern the Act of 1771, focusing initially on criticism of the role of local JPs,[131] then on a pamphlet issued by Lord Sheffield. Sheffield's proposals are minutely criticised by Corrie in a 74-page pamphlet of dense argument on *Considerations on the Corn Laws*, and Corrie also sent lengthy proposals for *Heads of Provisions for encouragement of tillage, navigation and manufactures, with remarks*. He published versions of these and other letters for general distribution. He also sent a heavily annotated copy of Sheffield's proposals with his own comments, and comments from James and Shoemaker, of Philadelphia, against the Corn Bill.[132] Much of this appears to have been prepared with others, particularly with the Glasgow chamber that was also lobbying against the Corn Laws very actively at this time.[133] The Bristol Venturers were also lobbying, but unfortunately do not refer

127 BL Add MS 38301 f. 42, 47; letters from Hawkesbury to Henry Wilckens 23 Sept 1789, 25 Jan 1790.
128 BL Add MS 38225, f.36, 106; letters from Henry Wilckens 11 Feb 1790, 24 March 1790.
129 Minutes of the Committee on Trade in response to Samuel Green secretary of the Liverpool chamber of commerce; 19 Oct 1790, f.179; 22 Nov 1790, f.185 (BL Add MS 38392); 23 March 1791, f.49–50; 28 March 1791 f.56 (BL Add MS 38393); Brown was a member of the Liverpool Committee of Trade.
130 Letters from Edgar Corrie; 15 Aug 1791, 2 March 1792; BL Add MS 38227, f.14, 268–271.
131 Letter from Edgar Corrie 1 March 1791; BL Add MS 38226, f.73.
132 Letters and pamphlet from Edgar Corrie: BL Add MS 38226, f.290–338, 25 Sept 1791; letters: BL Add MS 38227 f. 14, 21–6, 98; 15 and 25 Aug 1791, 18 Oct 1791. See also Liverpool Athenaeum, Misc. Papers 38, p 5ff.
133 Glasgow chamber minutes 2 January 1787, followed by an expensive lobby campaign up to 1790.

to Liverpool's efforts. The fact that Corrie and Wilckens, covert aboli-
tionist and public anti-abolitionist, both seem to be leading chamber
members in the 1787–92 period, suggests that the conflicts that were
aroused by the slave trade issue may have abated.

Another important issue in 1790–2 was again government proposals
for Free and Open Trade with the West Indies and Ireland. Having lost
the Irish propositions in 1784, Pitt attempted again to find a solution.
Green was contacted by the London Africa Committee in 1790, and was
asked to provide support for resisting this.[134] There is no record that he
replied; as noted before, the chamber members appear to have
supported this proposal, whilst the Corporation, its committee of trade,
and John Tarleton resisted it.

Further items of correspondence record that Samuel Green was still
secretary in 1791–2. On 30 July 1791 he wrote from the chamber to
Henry Taylor at North Shields supporting their proposal for "a floating
light at the north end of the Goodwin Sands; and a light on Longshore
Point, instead of the North Foreland light". In further support Green
also sent a memorial to Trinity House at Deptford Sound.[135] Later, in
1792, "Samuel Green, secretary to our chamber of commerce, brought
to me for inspection, a pamphlet, price sixpence, with a letter dated
North Shields, August 9 1792", which related to mooring practices of
colliers on the Tyne, recommending a method for keeping "ships to
leeward of their anchor".[136] This is the last recorded reference to Green
as chamber secretary that has been found.

[134] Africa Company to Samuel Green, 24 April 1790; TNA T70/70.
[135] *A Narrative of the Circumstances which led to fixing the lights in Han' Gatt, the light at the
Goodwin, ...,* James Phillips, London, 1796, pp 46–7.
[136] Reported in William Hutchinson, mariner, *A Treatise on naval architecture ...,* 4th edition, Billinge,
Liverpool, 1794, p 110.

8

The chamber 1792–6, after the death of Samuel Green

A major problem for the chamber must have emerged when, on 13 November 1792, Samuel Green died, aged 64. The newspapers stated that Green "possessed a solid and discriminating understanding considerably cultivated by literature and general knowledge. And the assiduous employment of his time and talents, for the commercial advantage of this town, must ensure him the reward of honourable esteem".[137] We also know from the Corporation minutes, that awarded him compensation for his slave trade opposition,[138] that "he was a zealous and faithful servant to his employers who reposed in him unlimited confidence ... his service ... greater [than could have been derived] from a common clerk inasmuch as his experience and situation made the more valuable and certainly stamped his proceedings with the greater respectability". The Corporation minutes describe his dedication and unique role: "It appears ... that Mr Green has been indiscriminately called upon in Liverpool for many years past by all descriptions of mercantile persons whenever official statements of facts or other written documents were necessary to be transmitted to

---

[137] Gore's General Advertiser, 15 November 1792.
[138] Common Council, minutes of 5 December 1792.

public offices in London to obtain redress of grievances or to remove temporary commercial inconveniences."

Given this critical role, filling Green's place would be difficult. Indeed it seems that his death left a vacuum for the chamber, which was temporarily filled by the elected chair and committee: there are no papers indicating that another secretary was appointed. Unfortunately, the reporting of the chamber had become erratic after 1787, and there are no records of elections to allow us to be sure of the evolution after Green's death. This makes the tracing of any chamber archives even more difficult after this date since we have to rely exclusively on correspondence that is primarily personal rather than written on behalf of the chamber.

Accommodation with the Corporation

One consequence seems to have been that the chamber members and the Corporation began even more actively to accommodate each other. In 1792–3 the mayor, Clayton Tarleton, brother of chamber member John, reformed all the committees of the Corporation. This resulted in extension of the committee of trade to a body of 13 members, three of whom were known or probable members of the chamber, and additionally one (Joseph Brooks senior) was strongly connected to the chamber. The reform certainly offered appeasement to the chamber members, and was simultaneous with the Corporation recognising Green's efforts with a payment for his services over the slave trade. There was, therefore, the scope for the committee of trade to take on the chamber's role, directly under the Corporation. This certainly seems to have been Clayton Tarleton's objective, since the Corporation minutes record his very personal intervention on behalf of Green. But it is doubtful that this succession strategy would have satisfied all chamber members, particularly the die-hard opponents of the Corporation, or opponents of the Tarletons, such as the Heywoods and Rathbones. In any case the committee of trade itself soon declined, ceasing to meet after May 1794. Hence, the period after late 1792 may have seen some of the chamber's activities merged into the Corporation or its committee of trade, but this could not have been the whole story.

John Tarleton takes over?

Another line of development came from John Tarleton (jun), Clayton's brother, where there is some indication that he sought to become chair, or chief facilitator, of the chamber. It is through him that almost all the approaches to government are channelled after Green's death. He took up a seat in 1792 as MP for Seaford after a contested result. Seaford was not his most desired option, for it appears he continued to seek to build support in Liverpool to transfer his seat in due course. This encouraged him to become very active for Liverpool mercantile interests. He wrote numerous letters over 1793–6 to Pitt and Lord Hawkesbury. His only previous political activity was as lead delegate for the Corporation in 1787–9 over the slave trade.[139] His letters are generally framed as coming "at the request of the merchants of Liverpool", or reporting that "at a meeting of merchants". Whether or not John Tarleton had any formal role with the remaining chamber members is unclear, but he was certainly able to insert himself as a critical intermediary for the Liverpool merchant community and became their main voice at Westminster. This allowed him to exercise a very personal influence, and opened the way for conflicts.

The 1793 banking crisis

With or without John Tarleton's influence, in March 1793, only four months after Green's death when a residual of the chamber must have still existed, the chamber members seem to have played a critical part of the local response to the failure of Caldwell's bank that had occurred at the end of February. This is not surprising as Caldwell was a member, and many of the other members would have had deposits with him. A petition from 122 merchants called for the Corporation to obtain a loan from the Bank of England. The probable role of the chamber is indicated by the establishment of a committee of six merchants "from the merchants at large", which contains four known chamber members, to work with a committee of the Corporation containing one known chamber member, who jointly drafted, lobbied and achieved success in the parliamentary Act to support the Corporation issue of loan notes to overcome the credit shortage.[140] This dual structure demonstrates the continued separation of the Corporation from the totality of the merchant community, for which whatever rump of the chamber still in existence provided some source of leadership, at least in terms of personalities appointed to the committee.

---

[139] Though, as noted earlier, his father had written to Pitt in 1784 (opposing open trade with Ireland and the West Indies), possibly to open an avenue with the new government.

[140] Common Council minutes, 20 March 1793: the Corporation Committee was Clayton Tarleton (mayor), Thomas Earle, William Crosbie jun, George Case, Joseph Brooks, and Richard Statham (all except Statham were Committee of Trade members); the Committee of Merchants (which was probably the chamber or the rump of its influence) was John Brown, Edward Falkner, Richard Walker, Thomas Hayhurst, Thomas Leyland and Jacob Nelson (four of whom were chamber members). Also see Hughes, 1906, pp 144–157.

The chamber membership, of course, could have been only part of the rescue, which was underpinned both by the Corporation, and most critically by Heywood's bank, since it was this that raised most of the additional credit required through the Bank of England and national Exchequer Bills.[141] Indeed' without Heywoods, the Corporation would not have been able to satisfy the Bank of England's requirements. For this the leadership of the Heywood chamber members, and the increasingly close relationship they had with the Earles, was critical. The initial Corporation plan for a loan had to be dropped in favour of issuing loan notes for which bank support was needed, both locally and nationally. Benjamin and Arthur Heywood, and Thomas and William Earle were critical to assuring both the Bank of England and the government that the Corporation loan notes were viable; indeed it is the Heywoods and Thomas Earle who signed most of the notes.[142] It appears that the merchant's committee was actually entirely a group of the residual chamber's committee, whilst the Corporation's committee was drawn almost entirely from its committee of trade. Interestingly and surprisingly, John Tarleton, initially unsuccessfully opposed this Bill in the Commons, against the efforts of these committees, and against his brother Clayton Tarleton as mayor.[143] This was presumably because of Pitt's initial opposition to the Bill and John Tarleton's efforts to stay close to the government.

Debt and taxes

One of the main areas of later concern for the Liverpool merchants was American trade and debts, an issue that had been one of the chief focuses of chamber lobbying in 1774–5, and became critical after American independence in 1776. A series of approaches directly to Pitt was made by Liverpool beginning in March 1795. This coincides with similar activities from London, Glasgow and Bristol. Clayton Tarleton, mayor, as well as John Tarleton, presented the case to Pitt.[144] The earlier claims by the chamber were revived. They were exacerbated by a new grievance over the destruction of British (and American) vessels by Earl Howe as Admiral in the West Indies to save them falling into French hands in June 1794. The pre-1776 debts, that had not been dealt with, were "ruining" some of the merchants.[145] This lobby eventually led to

---

[141] Hyde et al, 1951, p 372; see also Gonner, 1896.

[142] See Baines, 1852, pp 494–5; Hughes, 1906; Hyde et al., 1951; Chandler, 1964.

[143] Hughes, 1906, pp 144–157; Thorne, *History of Parliament*; John Tarleton, DNB, 2004, p 786.

[144] Letters from Clayton and John Tarleton to Pitt, 23 and 26 June 1794; 24 March 1795; 18 May 1795; 5 June 1795; 21 July 1795, PRO 30/8/182 f.19, 26–7, 34–8.

[145] Some debts had been dealt with under the legislation to compensate loyalists in 1789, eg some of those of William Bolden and his associates: See Schofield, 1964, pp 126–7; PRO AO 12/54 pp 353–70. There is no record of any chamber involvement in these loyalist debt recoveries.

success. Adjudication of losses from Lord Howe's actions was under-taken by a committee chaired by Calverley Bewicke, a broker at Lloyds in London. John Tarleton pressed Pitt and Bewicke over these claims in April 1796.[146] The American debt issue was resolved by a treaty between the two countries, signed in Britain on 19 November 1794 that mainly concerned commercial settlement.[147]

Liverpool, along with the Manchester and Glasgow chambers, was also exercised about the local impact of the Salt Tax in 1795. The north-west bodies sought an equal playing field in level of tax with Scotland. Glasgow sought abolition. Liverpool was particularly concerned about the arbitrary distinction (as they saw it) between white salt and rock salt. White salt was imported essentially processed, whilst rock salt needed three months "to give the proprietors time to convey the rock salt to their respective works, … and cure it for sale … (but) *they pay the duty for the rock salt before it is removed from the mines.* Whereas the proprietors of white salt works only pay the duty *after it is made, dried and delivered for sale!*"[148] There was also liaison between the Manchester chamber and Liverpool in 1796 over convoys and related matters, where Thomas and William Earle are identified as the main spokesmen.[149] The Glasgow chamber history refers to the Liverpool chamber in 1798 in relation to convoying to the Baltic,[150] but it is not certain there was actually a chamber at this time.

The lobby against the East India Company

Interesting further insights into developments after Green's death are provided by the lobby of November 1792 concerning the renewal of the charter of the East India Company.[151] A printed letter and petition of a public meeting was circulated by Jonas Bold. This meeting was called by the mayor (Clayton Tarleton). Five of the committee of 12 (42%) were linked to the chamber, and Jonas Bold was a banking partner of Thomas Staniforth,[152] though it is claimed that William

---

[146] John Tarleton to Bewicke, copied to Pitt; PRO 30/8/182 f.46, 48.

[147] The treaty is referred to by Clayton Tarleton in his letter to Pitt 26 June 1794; PRO 30/8/182 f.19. However, this only began a long process: commercial settlements were not finally resolved until 1804.

[148] Letter from John Tarleton 17 December 1795 to Pitt, enclosing a letter from Nicholas Ashton of same date; PRO 30/8/182, f. 42–44; emphasis is original. The concerns continued: Wilckens developed a continuing lobby over these issues in 1798 and 1804: *Letters on the Salt Trade*, Liverpool Athenaeum, Misc. Papers 65.

[149] Manchester chamber of commerce minutes, 9 and 22 November 1796; John Rylands Library M8/1/1.

[150] Oakley, 1983, p 26.

[151] This was in many ways a revival of earlier campaigns by Liverpool, in 1729, 1768 and 1777: Pope, 1970, vol. 2, pp 448–9.

[152] Circular letter of 27 November 1792 and printed petition of 24 November; BL Add MS 38228, f. 151–3; the chamber members were Francis Ingram, Joseph Dalterra, William Earle, Nicholas Ashton, Thomas Hodgson junior; see also Brooke, 1853; Pope, 1970, vol.2, p 449.

Rathbone led the campaign.[153] That this lobby was not fronted by the chamber is surprising, since a similar lobby by Glasgow was.[154] It is perhaps a clear sign of the chamber beginning to disintegrate after Green's death, that it was becoming integrated into the Corporation under Clayton Tarleton, or that we do not know enough of the later chamber member names to ascertain the full extent of chamber involvement. But this lobby is also indicative of other emerging difficulties, since, when John Tarleton forwarded the printed resolution to Hawkesbury, he stated in his covering letter that if a petition was developed "I shall not fail warmly to oppose, being firmly convinced that this measure is brought forward at this crisis by a certain description or class of men merely with the view to embarrass government",[155] despite the petition being careful to state that "no motives of party whatsoever" were involved. Tarleton was clearly now playing to the government's tune, reasserting the old Tory bent of the Corporation 'families' against what he perceived as Whiggish merchants.[156]

Similarly, in February 1795, when Tarleton sent the resolution of a "committee to act for the shipping interests of Liverpool", which he was to present personally to Hawkesbury, he equivocated. This committee was chaired by Nicholas Ashton, and had five other known chamber members (Bolton, Cragg, Earle, Benjamin Heywood and Leyland), and one probable member (Backhouse) (35% of the total of 20).[157] This lobby against a "Bill for the better regulation and government of seamen in the merchant service" sought to fix maximum pay rates to reduce competition with the Navy. Tarleton's letter strongly implies that at his personal meeting with Hawkesbury he would again not support the lobby, playing to the government's line rather than those he was representing.[158]

Other concerns 1793–6

In June 1794 Tarleton raised the concerns of the 'merchants of Liverpool' about the actions of Charles Grey, army commander, and John Jervis, naval commander of forces attacking Guadalupe, Martinique and St Lucia. He refers to their "highly improper proceedings … aggression, extortion and violence".[159] By November he is requesting that the King

[153] Rathbone, 1913, pp.96–7.

[154] Glasgow minutes and chamber papers TD 1670/4/74; Report of Committee on the East India Trade, 25 December 1792.

[155] John Tarleton to Hawkesbury, 3 December 1792; BL Add MS 38228, f. 149–50.

[156] Compare Sanderson, 1977.

[157] John Tarleton letter to Hawkesbury, 13 February 1795, enclosing resolutions of the Liverpool Committee meeting of 11 February; BL Add MS 38377, f. 19–21.

[158] The Bristol Merchant Venturers also give little support to this Bill; out-letter to John Tarleton 31 March 1795; SMV/2/4/1/2

"order a restitution of the inglorious booty acquired by our commanders".[160] In 1794/5 Edgar Corrie was again active, writing letters to Pat Heron MP concerning Scottish distillery laws,[161] indicating that he may have been the chamber chair or vice chair at the time. Other references to the Liverpool merchants (but not explicitly to the chamber) occur in the Manchester chamber minutes as one of the bodies working with the Admiralty to structure the convoys which were used when war again broke out with France, in 1793.[162] Convoys were a particular concern of the Manchester chamber. The only explicit Liverpool reference to convoys that has been found is in an exchange between Clayton Tarleton, mayor, and Bamber Gascoyne MP in 1793 when Gascoyne transmitted a request from Pitt for a deputation from Liverpool to "point out the most effective means for protecting its shipping from attacks of the enemy".[163] Tarleton replied that "at a most numerous and respectable meeting of the merchants of this port", Mr Case, Mr Walker and Mr Richard Watt were nominated; "when I mention the names ... you will, I am confident, know ... that the Africa, West India, Baltic and coasting trade of this port are well represented".[164]

Liverpool chamber members were probably in the lead in promoting a Bill to regulate desertion of seamen from merchant ships in 1795/6 (again an echo of its earlier concerns in February 1777). The problem perceived was that sailors would sign up for a whole double voyage at Liverpool, but would desert in the West Indies "in order to extort high wages by the run in other vessels homeward bound, deserting in a like manner".[165] The draft Bill was presented through John Tarleton, who also approached Pitt, and became concerned when the Bill laid in Parliament "proposes no penalty on the seamen, it only aims at removing the temptation for him to do wrong ... the bill leaves every other point unchanged".[166] Tarleton also wrote to the Bristol Venturers for support, but they refused, a meeting of their merchants judging the proposals "not expedient".[167]

---

[159] John Tarleton letters to Hawkesbury 22 and 26 June 1794; BL Add MS 38229, f. 255, 342.
[160] John Tarleton letter to Hawkesbury 15 November 1794; BL Add MS 38230, f. 115–6.
[161] Edgar Corrie letters to Pa. Heron MP, 24 December 1794; 4 April and 4 June 1795; Liverpool Athenaeum Misc. Papers 38, p 181ff.
[162] Manchester chamber minutes, 1793; see also Helm, 1897; Redford, 1934, chapter 3.
[163] Bamber Gascoyne to Clayton Tarleton 9 February 1793 transmitting Pitt's request LRO 920 TAR/4/54.
[164] Clayton Tarleton to Bamber Gascoyne, 11 February 1793, LRO 920 TAR/4/56.
[165] Letter from John Tarleton to Pitt 23 April 1796 enclosing printed resolution of meeting at Liverpool, 13 April 1796: PRO 30/8/182, f. 51–2.
[166] Letter from John Cragg, 7 May 1796, sent by John Tarleton to Pitt, and draft Act: PRO 30/8/182 f. 55–60.
[167] Out-letter from Master of SMV in reply to John Tarleton, enclosing resolution of the Bristol merchants, 31 March 1795: SMV/2/4/1/2. Proceedings SMV/2/1/2/3, p 393.

Other correspondence from John Tarleton in the Chatham papers reveals the names of two further businesses that were probably chamber members. Tarleton wrote on behalf of John Cragg about the 1796 draft merchant seamen's Bill referring to concerns by "gentlemen of this committee" (probably the rump of the chamber of commerce).[168] The chamber member Jacob Nelson chaired a meeting in 1796 concerning seamen's desertion in the West Indies.[169]

Activity but tensions and growing division

This summary of development after Green's death shows continuing activity up to about 1796, led by what appear to be the Liverpool chamber's members, though perhaps not by a formal chamber as such. Although we cannot be certain of how the chamber itself was now constituted, the residual of its former members, or the rump of its committee, were certainly very active in most of the most significant of Liverpool's commercial lobbies over 1793–6. The focus of activity appears to have remained the same: international trade, convoys, seamen, domestic taxes, shipping quotas and embargoes. Key concerns of later chamber campaigns, such as the Corn Laws and East India Company, also began to emerge. Doubtless there were other concerns that may be discovered in other papers. But the key implication of the evidence from the sources currently known is of a continued and active chamber membership.

However, after the death of Samuel Green in 1792 there is considerable confusion in tracing activities and from this date tensions emerged. The 1792–6 letters of John Tarleton show him playing multiple roles as advocate for the city and the chamber members' interests, but also as MP and supporter of the government, which led to potential for confusion and conflicts of interest. At the same time the Corporation under Clayton Tarleton became much more supportive of many of the chamber's members and their interests. Both these developments would have increased confusion about representations, who was the main voice, would have undermined the chamber's remaining position, and led to disaffection of some members, which came to a climax in 1796 when John Tarleton put himself beyond the bounds of gentlemanly conduct of the day, as discussed later.

---

[168] John Tarleton to Pitt enclosing letter from John Cragg, both dated 7 May 1796; PRO 30/8/182 f. 59–60.
[169] John Tarleton to Pitt, 13 March 1796, PRO 30/8/182 f. 52.

9
The forces for chamber formation, and relationship with the Corporation

We have seen what the chamber did: but why did it start, and why then, in 1774? Then, as now, an idea was not enough in itself to get busy business people moving; they needed a real cause for action. The draft *Deed* makes clear that one of the key initial motives was the trade duty; and the target was the body levying it – the Corporation. Reforming the trade duty is the closest Liverpool's chamber came to an explicit statement of objectives. As a public document, the main purpose of the *Deed* was to encourage subscribers. To make the trade duty its initial and central focus must have been resonating with a major concern of that moment. In now trying to interpret how the chamber emerged we have to reconstruct why this concern was so prominent.

Phase 1:
The initial concept for a Committee of Trade
What can be clearly shown is that there was a very public conflict in early 1774 between the leading merchants, who established the chamber, and the Corporation. The merchants' objections were led by

John Dobson, who became the first chair of the chamber. The full detail of the Corporation's activities is beyond the scope of this book and some aspects will remain uncertain. However, it is clear that the trade duty was a central source of anger to Dobson and his colleagues. This duty consisted of town duty (a tax on imports and exports based on the origin and tonnage of the ship) which had amounted to £1,023 for 1760, and dock dues (amounting to £2,383 for 1760). The dock dues fell on all ships and cargoes using the docks; but the town duty fell on all shipping whether or not it was in a dock or using another legal quay, or merely transhipping cargo in the river (as occurred for much salt, coal and merchandise that arrived by ship in the Mersey from the Weaver, Sankey, Trent-Mersey and other inland routes). The town duty was deeply resented, as it was a fee for which no service was provided.

These fees had been increasing rapidly; the town duty reaching £4,536 and the dock dues £45,880 for 1774.[170] Both the town and dock dues fell mainly on the long-distance traders.[171] The dispute over the fees was both as to their level, and to the equity with which they were raised (especially that some merchants appeared to be allowed to treat it as a voluntary duty, and freemen in any case were exempt from some parts).[172] The Corporation later fought a legal case on whether freemen from London were exempt, and the legal briefing on this case reveals the tensions involved.[173]

The 1774 dispute appears to have followed from a proposed petition that the merchants were considering submitting to parliament on about the 16 February. The text does not seem to have survived but other reports suggest it was seeking to gain control of the Corporation's "trade duty laid on goods passing through the Port" to set up an economic fund. A public meeting, called via the newspapers on 25 February 1774,[174] states that this was for "merchants and traders who subscribed the petition to parliament to raise a fund to be applied to the encouragement and support of commerce desired to meet on Saturday at 9.00 at Wrigley's Great Room". This all suggests that a proposal had been under consideration for some time, and it becomes clear that this had been for a co-operative scheme between the chamber proponents and the Corporation which was contained within a draft *Deed* that had been under discussion.

---

[170] Smithers, 1825, p 184; Baines, 1852, p 431; 447 and appendices; Touzeau, 1910, II, p 851; see also Hyde, 1971.

[171] Like the light dues, the dock dues varied with tonnage: from 2d per ton for ships from St. David's Head to Carlisle; to 1s. per ton from Newfoundland, Greenland, Russia and Baltic; to 2s per ton from the West Indies, America, Europe within the Mediterranean, Asia, Africa and Cape Verde; BL Add MS 38351, f. 200.

[172] Touzeau, 1910, II, p 554.

[173] LRO Holt Gregson papers 942 HOL/19, pp 57–9

[174] Williamsons Advertiser, 25 February 1774.

Growing friction and breakdown of co-operation

The petition proposal seems to have been the result of the merchants' impatience with how the negotiations over the joint *Deed* were developing. They were going to go ahead on their own, directly to parliament. This led to a rapid response by the then mayor, John Parr.[175] He wrote a personal report, published on 16 February and repeated on 25 February and 4 March that:[176] "several merchants of this town propose immediately handing about a petition to parliament signed by the merchants, freemen and inhabitants, for leave to bring a Bill, this session, to lay a tax on all goods imported for the benefit of trade, as is alleged, and other purposes not explained, and speedily to bring in such a Bill contrary to the said merchants' public declaration, ... In order that they may have full time to *deliberate* on the scheme, I beg leave to recommend ... at present to postpone signing the petition". The mayor also apparently distributed handbills to the same effect.

The statements in the mayor's advertisement are repeated more or less verbatim in the Corporation minutes of 15 and 22 February, but the minutes go further: ordering if any "application be made or Bill brought into parliament that an opposition on behalf of and at the expense of the Corporation be made,"[177] and a committee of 12 aldermen plus the mayor, treasurer and town clerk was appointed "to manage such opposition".[178] None of the names of the committee listed can be identified as members of the chamber of commerce. This was the Corporation's insiders resisting efforts by outsiders to develop a joint committee using the town's duties.

Between 15 and 22 February a joint meeting with the "numerous merchants petitioners" was held with the Corporation's committee to try to resolve the discord. This joint meeting was clearly considering the joint *Deed*, which must have covered issues of governance and also the provision of a fund of £250 to support promotional activities for the city's commerce, which was to be based on the trade duties. The mayor had already published his letter on 16 and 25 February opposing this development and calling for postponement. Matters came to a head on 26 February. The Common Council met in the morning, and its minutes state that "several of the proposals now offered by the committee and proposers of the intended Bill for a tax on trade ... being in their opinion not proper to be complied with ... and if the petition to parliament ...

---

[175] Parr was a prominent slave trader and an member of the Africa Company, becoming its president in 1796.
[176] Williamsons Advertiser, 16 and 25 February, 4 March 1774.
[177] Town books; 352 CLE/TRA/1/2/10; see also Picton, 1886, p 236.
[178] Town books, p 132–3; 352 CLE/TRA/1/2/10: The named committee is Aldermen Gildart, Blackburn, Goore, Spencer, Hughes, Gregson and commoners Peters, Birch, Bridge, Brown and Clemens.

shall be presented contrary to the intent of the order of the Council the fund thereby established is or will be thereby void". The minute then went on to assert that it was still the commitment of the Council to represent the town's commercial interests.[179] This was effectively an ultimatum.

Divergent models

Between the morning Council meeting and the point when it was reconvened in the afternoon, a further meeting was held between the merchants and a representative of the Council, alderman John Sparling, who presented the Council's view. The Council's ultimatum, and the joint Deed as it then existed, were rejected by the merchants, who stated seven objections to the draft Deed. These objections were listed by the Chair of the merchants' committee, John Dobson, and were presented to the Council at their afternoon meeting. These objections are reported, over Dobson's name, in the Corporation Council minutes of 26 February. They are summarised in Table 4. Dobson's statement of objections is extraordinary for three reasons: first it shows how the thinking of those who were to become the chamber's leaders was developing; second, it shows the fault lines with the Corporation; and third, the fact that it has not been properly noted in subsequent histories demonstrates how the chamber's early history has been obscured by the Corporation's active resistance.[180]

The merchants' position was clearly in favour of a process of open governance and elections, not restricted to freemen, with a relatively large committee, and a turnover of chair and committee members on a regular basis. The trade duty was to provide a levy with a minimum of £250, but could be raised if needed to £500 per year. And the merchants asserted that it was their right to levy a residue of the trade duty (the comment from the chamber's own *Deed* opening statement being that they believed the duty to be voluntary, and was ceded to the Corporation's only on their behalf, and with their agreement).

The Council, on the other hand, was not going to cede rights over the trade duty, wanted to restrict committee members to freemen, was clearly seeking to have a chair and members that might continue indefinitely, as with the Council itself, and where the whole body could be voted out by a majority of those in attendance. This last point had

---

[179] Corporation Council minutes, 26 February 1774; LRO mf. 252 Min/CON I.

[180] It is notable that James Touzeau, 1910, pp 553–7, who was a former town clerk, and Picton, 1886, p 236–8, on whom so many rely as sources, do not report these objections fully, nor record the name of John Dobson as chair, nor Sparling as the source of some of the tensions. Indeed neither Touzeau nor Picton ever mentions the chamber, despite other minute books of the Corporation referring to it, of which they should have been aware.

Table 4 The objections to the Corporation's proposals for the use of the trade duty, specified by John Dobson, Chair of the Committee of Merchants (Reported in Corporation Council minutes, 26 February 1774; LRO mf. 252 Min/CON I)

1st	"An improper mention is made of the residue of the trade duty … if it does not make clear its very existence besides that this residue is not the property of the contracting parties."
2nd	"The mode of electing committee men tends to keep up that unhappy distinction of Party in the town which is the avowed intention of this negotiation to prevent, and the excluding all merchants, who are not freemen burgesses, from voting for the choice of committee men appears a high injustice to many of the most respectable contributors to that very fund that supplies our expenses and whose extensive traffic enriches the community. We think the right of electing committee men should belong to every person paying twenty shillings annually to the Town's Duty, … or who pays duties to the amount of fifty pounds annually or who is an owner or part owner of some ships belonging to this port."
3rd	"Mr. Sparling being one of the Council it is suggested, can't with propriety be named a trustee in the Deed – Though gentlemen who are named with him, wish a few more gentlemen may be nominated in the Trust, from motives of delicacy."
4th	"A small committee was found injurious in the application of the former trade duty. This evil can be guarded against by increasing the number to sixteen, eight of whom, shall be empowered to act and constitute a sufficient committee", with notice of meetings to be given and a process specified to act in urgent matters.
5th	"The retiring chairman may eventually continue the office in that body to which he belongs ad infinitum – The chairman should be chosen annually by drawing lots except the committee be unanimous in the choice of one of their body."
6th	"By the clause respecting the continuance of this grant, its existence may cease whenever a majority of voices in the committee shall so determine – The consent at least of every member of the committee seems indispensably necessary on a decision of such importance.
	It's thought necessary that the committee chosen by the merchants shall constitute a sufficient committee and be vested with every power of a full committee chosen by the Council and merchants in case the Council shall neglect to make their election on or before the twelfth day of March – and that the committee chosen by the Council shall have the same powers of acting if the merchants shall neglect to choose their number of committee on or before the same day."
7th	"If £250 shall be found insufficient by the committee they should have a power to call for any sum not exceeding £500 annually …
	Those gentlemen who have a right to vote in Council for committee men should be excluded from all right of voting in the choice of the business committee men or interfering in such election.
	The place appointed for the Committee Room is quite too small."

particular edge since the fourth objection tells us that the committee was to be composed of two groups, eight from the Council and eight from the merchants at large. The eight Council members, plus any one of the others that they could influence, could thus control the body, including its abolition. This concern as to loss of control is carried over into the seventh objection, where the merchants sought to exclude the freemen from acting as part of both electorates. The reference to the size of the Committee Room also indicates that they were concerned about being squeezed out and unable to attend meetings properly; it may also indicate a desire that committee meetings be held where other members could also attend and spectate, as in most other early chambers. The comments on 'Party' confirm a further concern: resistance of the merchants to the control by the Council of the parliamentary franchise on behalf of government (achieved through its election of freemen). The merchants wanted an *independent* voice that could lobby government without fetters from government influence.

The joint Deed that had been under consideration does not seem to have survived, but there is sufficient detail here to show why the merchants were not going to accept it. And the resistance of the Council is equally clear, since the merchants wanted to usurp (or as the merchants saw it, retrieve) part of the trade duty and put freemen on an equal standing with other merchants. This challenged the Council's ancient rights and the whole structure of patronage of 18th century Britain, including manipulation of parliamentary elections. Thus, this was not just an issue about the trade duty, or even about forming a chamber of commerce. For the Council, as stated in the 26 February minutes, it was about the control of local state power, and who was to speak on behalf of Liverpool: "the mayor and Council ... assembled still retaining and meaning in all things to show a due regard to the commonwealth of this town, will always on proper occasions administer such aids to the commercial interests of this town".[181] Its minute of 22 February also recognised: "that it is frequently necessary to send up deputies, and that resources are wanted to defray the expenses of deputies attending parliament ... concerning that and other purposes relating to, and to the promotion and support of such trade".[182] The point of contention was the representation of the city: who would speak to ministers and parliament, and the costs of doing so. At the end of the day this was a clash over who was to be the 'voice for business' in the city.

[181] Corporation minutes, 26 February 1774; also Picton, 1886, p 237.
[182] Corporation minutes, 22 February 1774, 352 CLE/TRA/1/2/10.

The Corporation's minutes of 26 February show that the "objections or proposals [from Dobson] being this day brought in by Mr Sparling as he declared from the assembly of the petitioners ... after being deliberately read over by the town clerk three several times to the Council and after many debates thereon and the questions put thereon" the Council voted "nem. con. against accepting them".[183] This account suggests some internal tensions in the Corporation, and that some were seeking a compromise. But the mayor, John Parr, who clearly already felt sufficiently confident to have published his rather misleading letter quoted above in the local newspapers on 16 and 25 February, was able to push through the rejection of the proposed committee; and he clearly had sufficient support to do so.

The proposal under consideration seems to have never had a title beyond 'Committee', or 'Committee of Trade'. In the Council minutes of 26 February it was referred to as relating to "the intended Bill for a tax on trade". It certainly does not seem at that time to have been considered as a chamber of commerce, and its constitution at that time had no resemblance to the Jersey or New York predecessors. These had no dual structure with local municipal Corporations, and were entirely independent self-governing bodies. Thus, if a chamber was indeed under consideration, it was being heavily compromised in the Committee proposal in order to attach the chamber idea to the trade duty. Hence, Liverpool's early chamber was running on two somewhat conflicting tracks, that the proposers might only have been faintly aware of at the time: one based on free elections and open governance; and the other based on seeking quasi-Corporation powers with rights to levy a voluntary tax. Jersey did manage to bring these two aspects together for a period, and New York had toyed with it, but it was an uncomfortable match, especially in an 18th century where Corporation powers were jealously guarded and were subject to extensive government influence through patronage. However, this was not the end of the story.

Phase 2:
The chamber emerges as an alternative

The Corporation had rejected a co-operative model with the merchants, based on a committee of eight from each. But the merchants clearly still felt sufficiently aggrieved to look for a different way forward. The Corporation's rejection, and the mayor's repeat of his report on 4 March, were inflammatory and elicited a response on 11 March. An anonymous

[183] Town books, pp 136–7; 352 CLE/TRA/1/2/10.

letter from 'A merchant of Liverpool' was directed at the mayor, which in its original rather complex punctuation was as follows:

"Sir, when you dispersed in handbills through this town your address to the inhabitants dated 16 February, charging a considerable body of merchants with duplicity, and a public *breach of faith*, your abuse passed unnoticed as it was concluded, that through misconception, or in misrepresentation you did not *then* know you subscribed and published a falsehood. – For this reason … they thought it unnecessary …either to confute your slander, or to reply to the charge as groundless and unworthy insinuation. It was also the determination of the gentlemen you impeached, to avoid every step that ever might *eventually* tend to foment any Party altercations, which they deemed your letter solely calculated and published to provoke. (- but since he has gone on spreading his abuse -) The Deputy Recorder of this town, who was sent by the council to oppose the intended application by the merchants to parliament; said – "He apprehended it was the intention of those who were anxious for the success of this scheme to apply for an act this session of parliament", when one gentleman arrived "*No*, not this session;" - upon which, the gentleman who first publicly moved this business, rose up, and said, "we do not yet *know* whether it will be applied for this session or not, - yet the mayor has gone on." … "Whenever … he can prove the calumny he has subscribed; he may be assured of knowing the author of this letter. The turpitude of uttering a falsehood recoils upon the position of the worshipful mayor of Liverpool." [184]

The mayor was seen as breaching faith on what had been understood to be the direction of previous discussions about a joint committee. He was also accused of distortion, arguing that the proposed petition for town dues would lead to an 'increased' levy, but 'A Merchant' claims it was to use part of the *existing* levy. Although we do not definitely know the writer of this letter, Dobson's previous position as chair of the merchants' committee, and the rather convoluted punctuation, which is reminiscent of the Objections, all point to Dobson. In both cases they reflect the spoken word and were probably taken down by a clerk (a common practice among the merchants); if so we almost have a record of Dobson speaking to us. He was clearly indignant!

[184] Williamsons Advertiser, 11 March 1774, emphases, brackets and punctuation as in original. The fact that John Dobson became the first chamber president may indicate that he was the writer of this letter.

Following the letter from 'A Merchant', a further public meeting was called in the Exchange of "gentlemen who have paid the trade duty" on 18 March.[185] It would appear that it was from this meeting that the chamber's own draft *Deed* emerged, dated 21 April. The timing all points to the proposal for a chamber being a response to having to find an alternative model after rejection by the Corporation of co-operative working. This was also the date of the 1774 general election, when William Meredith, who was seen as an opponent of the Corporation and the government, was re-elected as MP unopposed, with chamber prominent member Staniforth his leading supporter.[186] It is also clear that, from March, at least as an immediate strategy, the idea was abandoned of presenting a petition to parliament to 'retrieve' the trade duty as their 'voluntary' payment directed to a new body; or, as the draft chamber *Deed* states, to revive an "ancient association" of mutual supports. Although the *Deed* mentions this, the actual means of financing the chamber was from a subscription unrelated to the trade duty. Probably it became obvious to the merchants that they could not succeed in parliament against the opposition of the Corporation; and that to pursue it would require lengthy and costly litigation about where the fundamental rights to levy the duty lay which would have obstructed what appears to have been their immediate purpose – to set up their own body.

Subsequent to the Liverpool local newspaper exchanges with the mayor, on 8 March in the *Manchester Mercury*, and on 15 April in Liverpool, the establishment of the first Manchester chamber of commerce was reported[187] "to consider proper measures for the services and encouragement of trade of that town and neighbourhood a committee was appointed for these important purposes ... This committee has regularly met and adopted several measures relative to the present state of trade which, it is not doubted, will have most beneficial consequences. All their proceedings are minuted, and copies taken of all letters sent and received ... and the public are so fully satisfied of the great utility of this patriotic undertaking, that near two thousand pounds have been already subscribed for the support of the chamber of commerce in Manchester". The Liverpool chamber *Deed* was published shortly after, on 21 April 1774.

By March–April, if there was not already the model for a chamber in mind, nearby Manchester offered it. We also know that Manchester's development was in the minds of people like Benjamin Heywood, who

---

[185] Williamsons Advertiser, 18 March 1774.
[186] Staniforth hosted his celebratory dinner: Williamsons Advertiser, 19 March 1774.
[187] Williamsons Advertiser, 15 April, 1774.

included the 8 March Manchester newspaper cutting in his *Curious Papers*; while John Dobson, Liverpool's first chair, and Thomas Butterworth Bayley, the chair of the new Manchester chamber, appear to have known each other well enough to appear together at a public meeting in Lancaster a year later when American concerns became extreme (see further below). There were also the Jersey and New York chambers, Dublin Committee of Merchants, and other connections between the Greenland traders in Liverpool (chiefly Staniforth, though Heywood clearly also had some Greenland interest) and Jersey, as well as the trade connections with New York and Dublin, as routes for exchange of information that could have suggested the chamber concept. Attempts to evidence these routes of information exchange have so far failed, but it would be extraordinary if the chamber concept that existed in Jersey, New York and Dublin was not then known sufficiently to be used in Liverpool and Manchester.

A further area of grievance may also have been the Exchange building. This had been originally built by merchant subscriptions, but had been taken over by civic functions and meetings of the Corporation and magistrates. This was a source of public grievance later, when in 1793 'A Merchant' called for the Exchange to be extended and better enclosed to provide an improved environment for the merchants' activities.[188] They clearly felt relegated to a second-class position in 'their' building.

Why a chamber in 1774?

Another important question is why was this particular moment in early 1774 the occasion when the Liverpool chamber emerged? Disputes about the trade duty had clearly been rumbling for some time (and went back decades). The proposal to develop a joint Committee of Trade with the Corporation suggests that a specific accommodation was being negotiated at this time for a particular purpose. Was the breakdown between the two sides therefore just a matter of personalities? There was certainly the public intransigence and "public breach of faith", "abuse", "misrepresentation", "falsehood" and "slander" that 'A Merchant' claimed that the mayor John Parr had made. But Parr was not alone, since he received the support of the Council in its nem. con. rejection. So the intransigence was more widely shared.

There seem to be two ways of interpreting the situation. The first is that the Liverpool chamber initiative was part of a much larger issue about state authority, and how parliament was 'elected', that was then

---

[188] *Williams Advertiser* 10 January 1793.

being played out in the context of the American rebellion and the Wilkes Middlesex election affair. These issues became increasingly prominent as the government seemed intent on confrontation with the Americans. The general election of March 1774 was fought partly on the government's policy on America. These events are considered at length later, below, as part of the wider political activity of chamber members: but it is important here to note that the merchants may have been responding to the general challenge to the authority of a parliament that was judged to be embarking on a road to war that was becoming increasingly unpopular, a leading slogan of which was 'No taxation without representation'. Liverpool was a natural fulcrum where American issues would be in the front of minds. Hence, the breakdown of co-operation with the Corporation and agitation over the trade duty may have been last straws on top of various other frustrations.

However, there were also very local aspects, centred on John Sparling, that appear to have been the proximate catalyst against the background of the general challenge to the authority of 'elected' bodies. John Sparling's position is intriguing. He was the go-between of the Common Council with the committee of merchants on 26 February. Yet it was he who was explicitly rejected in Objection 3 by the merchants, as someone who could not "with propriety be named a trustee in the Deed". There is no comment on why Sparling was unacceptable, but there could not be a clearer statement that he was. His detested position appears to derive from his conflicts of interest on land development; an issue that is perfectly comprehensible in a modern context.

John Sparling and his land

John Sparling was a partner with William Bolden. Sparling and Bolden was by then a major merchant firm, mainly trading in America and Africa. William Bolden was a core member of the chamber's committee for most years 1775–85, but Sparling was never involved (as far as can be ascertained). Sparling had become a major Corporation Common Council member, and one of the elite Commissioners of the Watch, as well as connected to the Corporation inner circle of power 'families'[189] in a way that Bolden and most of the chamber members were not. He was to become High Sheriff in 1785 and mayor in 1790/1. Over 1772–4 there were many Council minutes relating to Sparling, who was by then an alderman, relating to purchase of his land. A transaction had begun in 1772 under Thomas Wilson as mayor, seeking to compensate

---

[189] Through the Shaws and Blundells, who were also shareholders in the firm: Schofield, 1964.

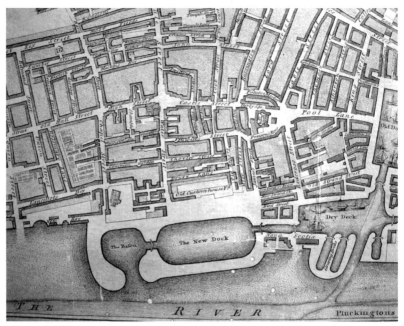

Liverpool, 1768 (Eyer)

Sparling for loss of land resulting from opening a new street. The Corporation's sought "Mr Sparling to leave open the end of the intended street at the North end of his pitch house on the South Shore which is to run through the ground now enclosing them down to the sea or river", paying him the costs of building a wall at the end of the said street and making a new slip.[190]

The probable location of Sparling's land can be deduced from the maps of the period, which show the intended streets that became Sparling St, Crosbie St and Tabley St, as shown in Figure 1. Sparling's land had been 'Mr Critchley's Garden' in 1769 (as shown in Perry's map), and hence had been only very recently acquired by Sparling. Part was now to be leased to the Corporation, based on decisions that Sparling was involved in making as an alderman. But matters became murkier.

In February 1773 the Council, now under Thomas Golightly as mayor, found that there were "several mistakes in the lease lately made to Mr Sparling of the Sea Strand by him now enclosing". There were four disputed elements: (i) "for or against his paying ground rent of twelve pence paid for the front of the old pitch house"; (ii) his obligation "to leave a street from Journey Lane through his new enclosure to his westward wall that now he is excused from making or leaving any such street there"; (iii) that "he was obliged to make the street running

[190] Corporation Council minutes, 7 October 1772.

from north to south fourteen yards wide along said pitch house prem-
ises ... [but it] be now only made twelve yards wide"; and (iv) that a
liberty he had in the lease "to go fifty yards deeper to the westward than
his present enclosure ... [should] be curtailed to twenty yards". The
Council ordered a new lease to be made with these changes. This occa-
sioned much discussion and led to new expenses for the Corporation.[191]
"On account of the cost and expense", a Council committee examined
his accounts of costs and expenses in November 1774, now under Parr
as mayor, and agreed to purchase the land for £1,450; in April 1775 he
was paid a further 5,000 guineas.[192] The true value of Sparling's interests cannot now be validly constructed, but it appears that he was being
over-compensated for land newly-acquired, which had benefited from

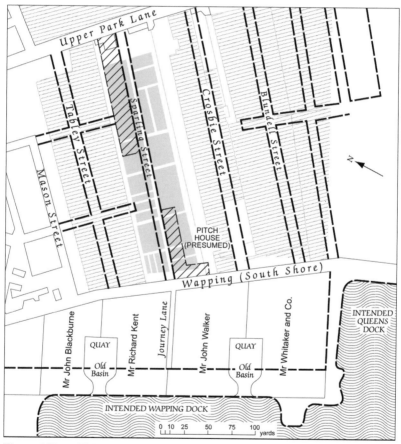

Figure 1 Map of John Sparling's land and adjacent areas: redrawn from maps by Eyer
1768 and 1785, and Perry 1769

[191] Corporation Council minutes, 3 February 1773, 6 and 18 October 1773,
[192] Corporation Council minutes, 2 November 1774; 5 April 1775.

his 'insider' position on the Council; the records show that he was in attendance at each of the relevant meetings.

The narrowness of Sparling St compared with the other adjacent streets is clear in Eyer's map of 1785, suggesting that, even after the new lease was drawn, Sparling managed to keep a larger area for development than originally intended. This restricted direct access to the shore, where a new route through land previously owned by Richard Kent is the presumed location of Journey Lane. This allowed merchants to access the strand where ships could be pulled up directly free of town dues.

It is notable that the main adjacent landowners in this area, Kent and John Walker, were chamber committee members and hence were very aware of, and directly affected by, Sparling's actions. The lease of Sparling's land therefore seems to have had all the ingredients necessary to inflame some of those who became leading chamber members. It may also be that the mayor, John Parr, was seen as offering personal favouritism to Sparling. Certainly the resolution of the 'mistakes' over the lease and Sparling's payment run over exactly the same period as the dispute with the merchants over establishing the chamber where Parr was seen as personally objectionable.

Sparling was to continue to be a concern later with the development of the Queen's Dock in the 1780s. In 1790/1 when Sparling was mayor, a petition of 1,028 local freemen were so incensed by the process of Council elections and the same names being elected, that they called for a 'Common Hall' to vote for new procedures, and requiring the Corporation's account books to be open and audited. Subsequent developments are complex, with a long legal case following in which Thomas Golightly, the treasurer, resisted opening the books. It is significant that the chamber leaders Arthur Heywood and the Rathbones were leaders of this campaign, although it was much more widely shared than the chamber's membership alone.[193]

Access to 'legal quays'

Perhaps as significant, however, is how the issue of Sparling's lease interrelated with another controversy over the right of the Corporation to levy duty on landings at legal quays that were separate from the new Corporation docks. A major flurry of concern arose in 1774 about fees on the east side of St George's Dock (built following a Dock Act of 1761, and newly completed in 1771). The disputed area was between the

[193] Summary in Brooke, 1853, pp 205, 399; Picton, 1903, pp 232–4. Rathbone role brought out in Rathbone, 1913; see also the Rathbone scrapbook; RP.II.4.16: Liverpool University Library.

bottom of Red Cross St and the bottom of Chapel St. The merchants claimed this land was a legal quay that pre-existed the new dock, and was outside the Corporation's jurisdiction. Hence, shipping and landing of goods should have been possible there, exempt from Corporation dues.[194] This dispute ran over the same time as the dispute about the chamber. The initial objections by the merchants were raised on 21 January 1774 and continued into December of that year, when it was confirmed by the town clerk that indeed the area was exempt from town dues.[195] This would seem unsurprising as it was the strand that formerly fronted the Custom House, which had been used as an open landing area from time immemorial. Hence, the merchants were right, the Corporation looked high-handed, and it was no longer able to charge the merchants docking there.

The dispute over the St George's Dock was separate from the Sparling land dispute, but both involved the access and use of landing places where the town dues were exempted. The Corporation's expansion of the docks cut across the previous rights of the shippers, and involved trying to levy more fees. Sparling's movement of walls and constraints on street widths were restricting access to the South Shore landing places, preventing the merchants making effective use of a free landing area. If anything was designed finally to goad the merchants into action it would be these shenanigans by Sparling to constrain their access, and the Corporation's efforts to bolster the trade duty, which appeared to be subsidising payments to Sparling for speculative land acquisition. This was all on top of John Parr's "abuse" and "slanders".

Sparling may also have been identified with the defeat by the Corporation in 1770 of a proposal by the Sankey canal's proprietors (of which the main parties affected were Case and Ashton, who were leading chamber members). It had been proposed to extend the Sankey to Wigan, but the Corporation was developing a rival Leeds–Liverpool canal scheme that left the Sankey isolated: "The Sankey Canal proprietors and their friends had been abandoned by official Liverpool."[196] Sparling was a leading alderman throughout this period of contention.

---

[194] As a result of an Exchequer Commission Report of 20 August 1723. It had been granted in lieu of 500 yards from the end of Red Cross St northerly to the Shilly Patch including the East side of the new St George's Dock; Jarvis, 1954, p 94–5.

[195] Jarvis, 1954, pp 94–5; Customs Letter Book entries 280 and 283, 21 January and 7 December 1774. The Customs seems also to have been restricted to taking fees only from the west side: LRO MIN/COM I 2/1: Committee of Trade, minutes 12 May and 5 June 1775.

[196] Barker and Harris, 1959, p 38.

Long-running sources of grievance

We can only conjecture on the specific issues that made Sparling so transparently *persona non grata*, but the development around his pitch house, and possibly the defeat of the Sankey, seem the likely causes that made him an unacceptable go-between in the negotiations for a joint committee of trade, and in any case would be further factors in inflaming relations with the Corporation. But, whatever the cause, the conflict of 1774 is not a unique example in Liverpool municipal history. The town dues and control of the docks were a source of earlier, and later, legal challenge.[197] These disputes were to continue for each stage of dock development, as with the next phase of the Wapping and Queen's Docks in the 1780s, shown in Figure 1.

Other analyses of the politics of Liverpool also demonstrate continual conflict with the small and self-electing body of the Corporation's mayor and Common Council, both before and after 1774.[198] The tension between the major merchants and the large number of freeman burgesses is referred to in Dobson's 2nd and 7th Objections. But the chamber cannot be seen as part of the general 'Whig' opposition to the 'Tory' Council that others have argued existed.[199] The majority of freemen would not be highly regarded by the chamber's merchants, since most freemen were small traders, labourers and sailors "with less than 10% composed of gentlemen, bankers and merchants"; for 1784 the electorate had about 250 of these groups, but these were only about 11% of the freemen electorate.[200] Moreover, most were elected in blocks of hundreds in the run-up to general elections. They were an outcome of the corrupt election system of the age that sought to maintain control of the Common Council and the election of MPs within closed 'family' interests. The merchants, on the other hand, were also mostly freemen, but almost all elected as individual cases usually after they had served apprenticeship in a Liverpool trading house, or as a result of their father's freeman status once they attained the right age. Virtually no merchant was elected in the large general election batches.[201] The merchants would have seen the bulk of the freemen beneath the status required for true freemen, created solely as election fodder.

The 'closed' nature of the Common Council is captured by Sanderson, who perceptively notes that, although "essentially the Outs were the same sort of people as the Ins", and the Council was "most

---

[197] In 1723, as noted by the Exchequer Commission; and in 1789 and 1830: Touzeau, vol. 2, pp 851–6.
[198] Muir and Platt, 1906; Muir, 1907; Touzeau, 1910; Sanderson, 1977.
[199] As argued eg by Sanderson, 1977.
[200] Aspinall, 1852, pp 102–3; see also Bradley 1990, p 67.
[201] This is clear from inspection of the freemen registers which give the time of election, and in most cases the occupation of the freeman; LRO 352 CLE/REG 1/1.

exclusive" and a "family party", this did not mean that there was not plenty of room for dispute at a personal level.[202] This would be especially true when it was believed that the Ins were incompetent, mostly seeking to feather their own nests and financial interests, or were more concerned to support the government than the town. While Sanderson states that "on important commercial issues the Corporation and the merchants at large almost invariably spoke with one voice and co-operated closely in sponsoring petitions to Parliament",[203] in the case of the formation of a chamber of commerce this was clearly not so. The analysis of the Corporation's minutes on this issue has also been obscured by Touzeau's statement of "a large amount of haze surrounding" the Corporation's proceedings of February 1774.[204] There was no haze; the mayor and Common Council's powers were challenged and they obstructed a compromise with the increasingly powerful merchant community of the city. There is also significant ground to challenge Sidney and Beatrice Webb's conclusion that Liverpool Corporation "impressed by its energy, and public spirit", or Muir and Platt's statement that the Corporation stood out like "an oasis of pure and reasonably competent government" in the pre-Reform period.[205] Significant parts of the business community were incensed with the Common Council, the mayor John Parr, and in some way particularly with John Sparling, and went ahead to find an alternative by founding the chamber.

Phase 3:
The Corporation's response: its own Committee of Trade

The Corporation did not ignore the chamber and, given that its legitimacy of voice was questioned, it is not surprising that it sought to compete. Even though the chamber had been successfully established, the Common Council established its own 'Committee of Trade', achieving agreement on this in December 1774, with its first formal meeting on 5 April 1775. It was formally referred to as a committee, but its minute book also occasionally refers to it as a 'Board of Trade'. It is also referred to occasionally by titles that overlap with the chamber: as the *Corporation Committee of Trade and Chamber* (25 July 1789) and *Committee of Trade Chamber* (13 July 1791). In each case these titles were used when writing to ministers. It is an interesting usage, since it suggests that the title 'chamber' had now acquired a level of

---

[202] Sanderson, 1977, p 70; Wallace, 1797; Menzies, 1972; see also Power, 1997.
[203] Sanderson, 1977, p 66.
[204] Touzeau, 1910, vol. 2, p 553, and following.
[205] Webb and Webb, 1906, p 482; Muir and Platt, 1906, p 138.

brand identity and status that it was useful for the committee to attempt to associate with.

The Corporation's committee was originally proposed to consist of the mayor and Bailiffs, seven or eight Aldermen, three councillors and the town clerk, to form a "Board of Trade and Commerce out of the Common Council".[206] But under its Deed, adopted 5 April 1775, it had a quasi-independent status and its own finances, with just seven nominated members of the Common Council, who elected their chair. There is no doubt that this was an attempt to show the merchant community that the Corporation could also set up an active independent voice, and it echoed some of the ideas in the Deed being negotiated with Dobson that was abandoned. The critical statement of purpose for the new body was: "their resolution to extend their corporate aids for the defence and promotion of all such trade and commerce as do or shall concern the interest of this town";[207] ie this was a parallel and rival voice to the then active chamber which had similar objectives.[208] There were no members in common. Touzeau interprets this as: "the Council realised their responsibilities and quickened their zeal with regard to fostering and protecting the trade of Liverpool when thus confronted with an attempt on the part of the merchants to take such matters into their own hands".[209] His account completely ignores the chamber then active, and how the two bodies actually evolved.

There is a surviving minute book of the Liverpool Committee of Trade and a set of accounts, which appear to have been almost entirely neglected in other historical analyses.[210] These show the committee to have existed from 1 April 1775 until 19 May 1794, meeting on 118 occasions. Its lifetime is tantalisingly similar to that of the chamber. Its founding Deed has the statement of purpose quoted above; a governance structure of seven Common Councillors appointed each year by the Common Council on the first Wednesday of April, with a formal minute book and accounts to be kept, and an annual report to be made to the Council. It was provided with £250 per annum to meet necessary expenses.

[206] In March 1775; Touzeau, 1910, vol. 2, p 556.
[207] Corporation minutes, 5 April 1775; Committee of Trade minutes, 5 April 1775; Touzeau, 1910, vol. 2, p 556; see also Picton, 1886, p 238.
[208] Checkland, 1952, p 58 and Barker and Harris, 1959, p 37 view the Corporation Committee on Trade, and the chamber, as the same body. This confusion is also copied in Pope's, 1970, vol. 2 pp 447–8 otherwise excellent account. The above account demonstrates they were not; they were founded at different dates, undertook different lobbies, had *no* early members in common as far as records allow; also while the Corporation Committee opposed the abolition of the slave trade, the chamber continued to have both pro- and anti-abolitionists.
[209] Touzeau, 1910, vol. 2, pp 553–5.
[210] The minute book is at LRO: 353 MIN/COM I 2/1; Accounts LRO: 352 TRE 5/111. Touzeau, 1910, vol. 2, p 557, states that "very little is recorded of … this committee", yet its full activities are recorded, which were extensive.

There is not space here to cover the full activities of the Corporation's committee, but a brief analysis serves to demonstrate that, after its early years of overlap in 1775–81, it mostly followed a different path from that of the chamber, focused on the docks and local issues. On four issues over 1782–5 it sought collaboration with the chamber through joint meetings. Hence, whatever the attitude of John Parr, John Sparling or other councillors, the members of the two bodies seem to have chosen some accommodation with each other after 1782. This may explain the very small amount of attention given to specifically local issues by the chamber, as noted in Table 2. As Sanderson observed,[211] all the individuals involved in local governance were business people, all busy people, so that it is likely they sought to accommodate and focus on different issues. There was, however, no overlap of membership between the two bodies until 1793 when the committee was reconstituted, and three chamber members were included: Thomas Staniforth, and probable members John Gregson, and John Shaw; Joseph Brooks (uncle of the chamber member Joseph Brooks junior) was also included; and James Carruthers, although never a committee member, acted as a delegate for the committee (and perhaps also for the chamber) on 7 July 1777. Notably, John Sparling was never a member.

Over its first three years (1776/7 – 1778/9), under its first chair John Blackburne, the committee was relatively inactive as a lobby (though actively taking various local actions). It initially opposed, then supported, the Chester lighthouse at Point of Ayr (coming into line with the chamber), supported the Smalls Bill (against the chamber), and exerted efforts to dampen the emerging movement to abolish the slave trade by sending delegates to the House of Commons. But in the last year of Blackburne's chairmanship, the committee became more politically active, with a major effort in 1778–9 in supporting the Council's petition to oppose a Bill to allow open trade with Ireland and the West Indies. It used Bamber Gascoyne MP and tried to get the support of other towns.[212] Perhaps the Liverpool committee can be credited with the organisation of the opposition to this bill since it was the vigorous petitions from most of these towns that derailed the efforts of Lord North's government to make progress on the Irish question. The absence of chamber actions on this Bill indicates that it was probably divided between different interests. On slavery and open trade it was unable to take a common view and had to preserve unity. The smaller body of seven Committee of Trade members reflected the Common Council's

---

[211] Sanderson, 1977.
[212] It wrote to Bristol, Lancaster, Chester, Preston, Wigan, Glasgow, Edinburgh, York, Leeds, Hull, Manchester, Warrington, Halifax and Whitehaven: minutes 15 April 1778.

view: to oppose moves to abolish slavery and to oppose open trade. This was predominantly a conservative protectionist body, like the Corporation itself.

William Gregson became the chair for six years, 1779/80 – 1784/5, with a short intermission over part of 1782/3 when John Brown was chair. This was a mixed period of relations with the chamber. Two actions, concerning navigation and the state of the estuary, have been noted elsewhere.[213] The committee also approached the Bristol Venturers in 1778, when John Blackburne jun, wrote as president of the committee, noting that they intended sending a memorial having seen French ships laden with sugar coming into the port. Interestingly they sent their letter to the Venturers via the Bristol mayor, as corporation to corporation. The Venturers responded with little interest and gave no support.[214] The Corporation committee wrote to the Venturers again in early 1779 opposing sugar exports from the West Indies entering via Ireland; the Venturers did not bother to respond.[215] There was also a significant amount of committee correspondence and actions up to 1781 about bounties on corn, Greenland ships, and fisheries. Hence over the period 1775–81 there was considerable overlap with the chamber's concerns about trade, and sometimes the two were at odds with each other.

Co-operation between the committee of trade and the chamber

However, after 1781 there seems to have been much more accommo-dation between the two. As noted earlier, there were joint actions on four issues, and one of these, on the fees and regulations of the Customs House, involved 11 joint meetings over December 1781 – March 1782. It would appear that at this time the two chairs, Gill Slater for the chamber, and William Gregson for the committee, were able to find a working relationship, which moved the committee to concentrate on more local matters. William Gregson had close association with several chamber members, particularly the Case family, and to several others through the powerful influence of Sarah Clayton and her family. John Gregson was a probable member, so that there was likely to be more sympathy for the chamber. Certainly it is characteristic of the period after 1782 that the committee became dominated chiefly with local

---

[213] Town Books; Touzeau, 1910, vol. 2, p 557; Picton, 1886, p 238–40.

[214] Letter from John Blackburne jun, 4 November 1778, mis-cataloged and externally mis-labelled as chamber of commerce; SMV/2/4/2/21 (12); out-letter 30 December 1778; SMV/2/4/1/1.

[215] Letter from John Blackburne jun. and Thomas Birch, Liverpool Committee of Trade, 22 February 1779; SMV/2/4/2/22 (6).

concerns: about the river, docks, local fisheries, Watchhouse, weighing attendants, Customs House, Excise House, repair and lengthening of graving docks, the Menai Bridge, and flats on the river.

The major exceptions to this division of labour were in 1785–6 when the committee opposed the Corn Bill and Tobacco Bill (against the Liverpool and Glasgow chambers), and from 1788 the committee spent much time and enormous resources on opposing the efforts by Dolben and Wilberforce in parliament to abolish the slave trade. The committee became one of the main vehicles used by the Corporation for marshalling its response to slave trade abolition, deputing a series of individuals to represent the case in London. Despite Green's role in this, he is not mentioned in the committee's papers, though he does write the committee's minutes over the short period of July–August 1789.

Thus the chamber and Corporation committee, after initial conflicts, appear to have found a means of coexistence. The major exceptions, after 1778, were the Bill for free trade with Ireland and the West Indies, Corn Bill, Tobacco Bill, and slave trade abolition.

Demise of the Corporation's Committee of Trade

The Corporation's committee of trade appears to have gone into abeyance after its meeting on 19 May 1794, when its minutes cease, and there is also no further Council minute of its existence. The committee had been reconstituted in February 1793, when the mayor Clayton Tarleton set up several new committees and regularised old ones "from the mayoralty of John Blackburne" (1760–1), who had died in 1788. The reconstitution enlarged the committee from seven to 13, with any five to make a committee quorum. Of the new membership, five came from the old committee, and three were definite or probable members of the chamber.

The abeyance of the committee probably occurred as a result of events that overtook it. Caldwell's bank had failed at the end of February 1793 and other banks had to struggle to survive. On 12 March 1793 the Corporation received the petition from the merchants calling for a Corporation loan scheme. The Corporation was forced to set up a joint committee of the Corporation and the merchants at large to petition for powers to raise its own Corporation loan notes to underwrite local credit and the banks. A Corporation Loan Office was set up on 27 May 1793. All this covered the period when the new members of the committee of trade had just been appointed. It is probable that the crisis of 1793 pushed the need for the committee to the margins. In any case, under Clayton's Tarleton's mayoralty much of the business of the former committees had been brought back directly under the Common Council so that the need for the committee was reduced.

Other areas of contention and reform: the Vestry

An important resonance of the conflict of the new chamber with the Corporation is reflected in the Liverpool parish Vestry. It is important to recall that until the Municipal Reform Acts of 1835 it was the Vestry rather than the Corporation that was responsible for most of what we would now recognise as municipal services: the workhouse, hospitals, prisons, fire engines, watchmen, civil defence of the town, police, poor law relief, etc. While the Corporation was rich, the Vestry was very poor.

The Vestry also underwent profound change in this period. After a long period of inefficiency and somewhat arbitrary exercise of its benevolent functions, a series of reforms were executed by Joseph Brooks (senior), after he became treasurer in 1768, a post he held for 20 years.[216] Brooks immediately changed the collection of the poor rate (which had been considerably in arrears and cost one-third of its receipt in collection costs through outsourcing, or 'farming'). Of critical importance was Brooks' initiative to build a workhouse in 1769, the costs of which were shared with the Corporation who owned the land. However, the argument as to who was to pay what proportion raged until finally resolved only in 1796, during which time the Heywoods' bank held the debt. Brooks also negotiated the transfer of the costs of paying for watchmen for the docks, which had been paid by the parish, to the much richer Corporation (as the trustees of the docks), to be paid out of dock duties. Disputes also raged with the Corporation over the level of dock duties liable for poor rating, and what was or was not liable to property rating; in 1786 the Vestry sought to rate the docks and shipping. Disputes continued into the early 1800s with a major court case fought in the 1830s.

The Vestry developments are significant because they echo the challenges to the Corporation by the chamber, in the same two fields of finance/competence and legitimacy. They are also significant because they show the emergence of a new generation of major merchants in Liverpool governance, and tensions with the old guard who ran the Corporation. Joseph Brooks senior, reforming treasurer of the Vestry, sought to encourage a new group of Commissioners (trustees for the Vestry) to stand for election, many of whom were chamber committee members. This period saw Thomas Staniforth and William Bolden

---

[216] The following summary draws from Peet, 1912; see especially pp xliv – lxiii, pp 227–9; see also Touzeau, 1910, vol. 2, pp 659–60, 671–2, 851–6.

Heywoods bank, Castle St., late 1790s

become key Vestry Commission members. At various times the chamber members Joseph Brooks junior, Edward Chaffers, Richard Kent, Ambrose Lace, Edgar Corrie and Thomas Hodgson also became Vestry Commissioners.

Infiltration of the Common Council

These developments suggest that a new group of leading businesses was emerging in the city in the 1770s, challenging the Corporation and Vestry managers and others of the old guard, frustrated with their inefficiencies, unhappy with the town dues they chiefly paid, but hungry for power and influence over the city's development. The Corporation was held by three 'families': the Tarletons (greens); the Earles, Rathbones and Curries (pinks); and the Gascoynes (blues). Aspinall interprets these as all sections of the Tory party; even the pinks were relatively moderate, but their self-styled 'colours' were nevertheless sources of deep hostility.

None of the known or probable chamber members were Common Councillors before 1774 (except Jonathan Blundell, probable member,

who was bailiff in 1764), although many were linked to the Corporation families. The chamber members, such as Leyland, Lake, Case, were
generally blues, whilst the Rathbones and Earles were pinks and hence
in conflict with the Tarletons in the Corporation.[217] The chamber
members who were family relatives of the Corporation 'families' appear
to have worked together in the chamber, at least up to 1796 when the
Tarletons fractured. But, as time progressed, some of the leading
chamber members did become Common Councillors, and this allowed
a closer working relationship between the chamber and the Corporation. It is probable that these internal voices helped to push the
committee of trade into a more co-operative mode after 1783. Thomas
Staniforth and Joseph Brooks became Common Councillors and
members of the committee of trade. Five or six chamber members
became mayors,[218] and several took on other municipal and 'establishment' positions;[219] two became High Sheriff, the 'crowning glory'
(Nicholas Ashton in 1770, and Edward Falkner in 1788).[220]

It is notable that the new guard came to power primarily under the
influence of the Tarletons, particularly Clayton Tarleton during his
mayoralty in 1791–3. It was this period that also saw Samuel Green
being rewarded and the committee of trade put in abeyance. Indeed
there was a remarkable run between 1789 and 1798 that saw five out
of nine mayors coming from the chamber's membership. Perhaps it
was this acquisition of other power bases and assimilation into the
Corporation and Vestry establishment that led to what might have been
a less active chamber in the 1790s.[221]

---

[217] Though the greens and blues would always coalesce to defeat the pinks: Aspinall, 1852, pp 102–4.

[218] William Hesketh, a probable chamber member, was bailiff in 1779 and mayor in 1783/4; Thomas
Smythe was bailiff in 1782 and mayor in 1789/90; Henry Blundell, a probable member, in 1793/4;
George Dunbar in 1796/7; Thomas Staniforth was bailiff in 1787 and mayor in 1797/8; Thomas
Leyland was mayor in 1798/9; Joseph Brooks jun was bailiff in 1784.

[219] JPs were Edward Falkner, Joseph Brooks junior, Nicholas Ashton, George Case and Thomas
Leyland; four became deputy lieutenants of the Lancashire: Nicholas Ashton, George Case, William
Earle and Edward Falkner; quoted in Pope, 1970, vol. 2, pp 471–2.

[220] Quoted in Pope, 1970, vol. 2, p 472.

[221] However, it would be wrong to see the chamber leaders as 'outsiders'; many came from long
established local dynasties. Also they were well represented on many other local bodies. Thus in
1774 the Gore *Directory* lists four chamber members among the 12 Commissioners for the Docks
(John Chorley, John Dobson, Alexander Nottingham and Edward Chaffers); there were five of the
18 Commissioners of the Watch (Thomas Case, Gill Slater, Joseph Brooks, John Dobson and
Benjamin Heywood); three of the 13 members of the Pilot Committee of which Joseph Brooks
was treasurer; and 5 of the 15 committee for the Seaman's Hospital of which Thomas Staniforth
was the president. Joseph Brooks was treasurer of the Dispensary established in 1778, and Nicholas
Ashton its president in 1779; In 1790 six of the 50 trustees of the Blue Coat School were chamber
members; 14 known chamber members were among the 96 subscribers to the Dispensary in 1778:
Boardman, 1871, p 42.

10
The members

Two important questions to answer with any lobby organisation are: who were the members, and how representative was the organisation of their interests. It is clear that, in Liverpool, personalities and their interests were key, so that knowing the membership is important to interpreting chamber activity. Unfortunately, for the first Liverpool chamber we have no complete membership list. But we have three other indicators of who were members. First, there is the known membership of the governing committee. With 21 members at any one time, plus the Honorary Secretary, and with a rotation each year (of variously seven or 14), the committee membership gives considerable scope to identify the leading and most active members. The complete list of known names of the committee over 1774–1787, which is shown in Table 2, numbers 61, inclusive of the secretary who as a major merchant must be assumed to be also a member.

A second source is those individuals who represented the chamber in 1775 in the lobby on parliament, John Walker and Ambrose Lace, named in the *Abstract*. There are also the two names mentioned in Tarleton's 1795–6 correspondence with Pitt (John Cragg and Jacob Nelson). These can all fairly confidently be assumed to be members. This brings the total of known members to 65.

A third source is a list held in Benjamin Heywood's *Curious Papers*. These contain a newspaper cutting of the loyalist petition of 6 October 1775. As we shall see later, this was a particularly divisive petition in Liverpool, and Heywood went through the list annotating names in several different ways. One annotation puts the letter 'M' next to some of the names. He does not give a key to this (as he does for his other annotations), and it is probable that the 'M' indicates chamber members. In corroboration of this, there is no known chamber member in the list (from the 65 derived above) who does not have an 'M' against his name.[222] But there are 23 additional names who may be chamber members. For purposes of the discussion here these names are referred to as 'probable' members, as listed in Table 5. Until further information is available, these are separated as 'probable' rather than definite members in all the discussions.

Table 5 List of additional 'probable' members of the Liverpool chamber in 1775: derived from Benjamin Heywood's *Curious Papers*, annotation of newspaper cutting of 8 October 1775 having the letter 'M' (excluding those already known as members and marked with an 'M')

Appleton Samuel	Jones John Chambres
Backhouse Daniel	Kelly Samuel
Black Patrick	Kewley Philip
Blundell Jonathan	Mason William
Bootle William	Mears William
Dunbar Thomas	Ormandy William
Grayson Anthony	Parke Thomas
Gregson John	Parker John
Grime Richard	Shaw John
Grimshaw Robert	Speers William
Hesketh William	Tuohy David
Holland Nemiah	Weatherherd Christopher

Size of the membership

The absence of a full list means that we can only estimate the size of the chamber's membership, but it important to attempt this in order to assess inclusiveness and representativeness. One guess can be derived from the 'probable' members noted from Heywood's *Curious Papers*.

[222] The other possible interpretation is that 'M' means merchant, but other cases in the list this is shown as 'Merch', except in two cases there is 'timber M' and 'wine M'. These two cases are not included in Table 5 since these clearly denote merchant. This ambiguity, however, is the main reason to be cautious about the 'probable' members.

There are 23 of these. There are also 16 *known* members listed in the same newspaper cutting. The known members listed are 24.6% of the total known members. If we treat the 23 probable members as 24.6% of the total probable, we reach a figure of 93 that would be probable members if similar proportions had signed or not signed the petition. Adding these to the known members (65) gives a total of 158.

This is no more than a guess, but it is in line with other chambers of the time. For example, Glasgow chamber had 218 founding members in 1783, and 131 by 1790; Edinburgh had 100 in 1785; Dublin 109 in 1783.[223] The Liverpool American chamber, a more specialist body, had 53 founding members in 1801–2.[224] Hence, a membership of about 100–160 in Liverpool is likely, if it was broadly comparable with similar cities.[225] Comparing this estimate with directory information (see later, below) suggests that the chamber was about 7–8% of all businesses, and 10–18% of the significant business community. This is again comparable to similar cities, and is remarkably similar to the market penetration of modern British chambers. It suggests that Liverpool's chamber was similar in representativeness, in terms of scale, to comparable organisations then and now.

Firm size, structure and organisation

A second issue is how far the 'interests' of the members represented Liverpool business as a whole. The known membership of the chamber is assessed in Appendix Table A.2 in terms of the type of business activity in which each member was involved, the field of trade or markets chiefly concerned, and the form of business organisation used. Appendix Table A.3 supplements this with analysis of the 23 probable members. The information on each business is derived from the contemporary trade directories heavily supplemented by other analyses of the Liverpool business community. This can be used as only an approximate guide since the records are at best partial. Also, since many businesses changed their form or markets several times, a single comparison date of 1780 is used, which is a point mid-way through the period covered by the committee membership information, and a date for which two directories are published.[226]

The composition of Liverpool chamber's members is clear from the Appendix Tables: most were merchants, shipping, or trading businesses.

---

[223] See Bennett, 2011, Appendix.
[224] Minutes; LRO 380 AME/4.
[225] In which case the 65 known members identified in this book are a large proportion of the total.
[226] Gore's and Bailey's; three members Cragg, Nelson and Bolton are referred to after 1786, and hence 1790 sources are used.

But manufacturing was also represented, particularly in sugar processing, pottery, glass, mining and rope-making. There were also banking, insurance, and local distribution businesses. Many businesses covered several activities, across manufacturing, trade and commercial activity. Case, Dobson, Earle, the Heywoods, the Hodgsons, Ingram, James, Leyland, Slater, Staniforth and the Tarletons appear to be the most diversified. Most of these were among the most continuous members of the chamber's committee (see Table 2). Hence, the chamber membership covered several leading sectors and was quite diversified.

An attempt to analyse more systematically the sector composition is given in Table 6. While any simple classification must be treated as only approximate given the information available and complexity of the businesses, this breakdown demonstrates five key features. First, most chamber member businesses were indeed sectorally diversified. The main diversification was between simple merchanting and shipping. This is to be expected given earlier analyses of Liverpool's shipping which show it to be very strongly interlocked with the merchants, owned 80% by them. However, the much higher level of interlock in Liverpool than in London (50%) or Whitehaven (15%),[227] was clearly reflected in the chamber's leading members. Diversification was also broader: one-fifth of all known members that were merchants had diversified also into manufacturing, and a further quarter into banking/insurance. For probable members, moves into banking are smaller, but the general level of diversification is similar. The diversification appears to have been driven by hopes for broader investment returns. For example, merchants expanded their interests into pottery, where the manufacture became heavily dependent on them both for investment and export markets. The Gregson banking records state that, "every merchant of note in Liverpool had some interest in a pothouse".[228] Other merchants were involved in manufacturing salt, sugar baking, brewing, and trades associated with shipbuilding and maintenance such as rope manufacture.

Second, the merchant and shipping concerns, generally combined, were dominant among committee members. Liverpool was a great port for its region and this is reflected in its chamber membership where over 95% of its known members and 90% of probable members had some direct shipping interest. Third, banking and insurance were strongly interconnected with chiefly merchanting, and/or with manufacture. This reflects the origins of 'country banking' in general, where

---

[227] Jarvis, 1969, p 417.
[228] Boney, 1957, p 144; p.5, n.2.; quoting the Holt and Gregson papers; also quoted in Gatty, 1882, p 4.

Table 6 Sector industrial composition of Liverpool chamber of commerce members in c.1780. City composition by sector from count of local directories in 1780–1; from these sources it is impossible to separate different types of merchants

	Known members (no)	Known members (%)	Probable members (no)	Probable members (%)	City (%)
Manufacturer primarily	1	1.5	-	-	23.5
Warehousing primarily	1	1.5	-	-	5.8
Merchant solely or primarily	13	20.0	10	43.6	}
Merchant/trader/ shipping combined	21	32.3	5	21.7	} 37.4
Manufacturer and merchant/shipping combined	14	21.5	5	21.7	}
Insurance/banking combined with manufacture or merchanting/ shipping	16	24.6	1	4.3	3.4
Other	0	0	2	8.7	29.9

the commercial banking function grew from the general practice of holding trading credits. It also appears that almost *all* the major banking interests of Liverpool at this time were among the leading members of the chamber.[229]

Fourth, as far as can be deduced from commentaries in contemporary sources, many of the businesses which were leading chamber members were also the major businesses in their fields. At least 26 (40%) of the known members, but four (17%) of the probables, are referred to as 'major' shipowners, bankers etc, in their fields in contemporary records.[230] Another indicator of their recognised importance is that 18 (51%) of the 35 flags of the main merchants shown on contemporary pottery mugs and jugs were known chamber members, and three were probables, (60%) in all.[231] The critical importance of the major merchants is evidenced in one account of Messrs Earle: "to whom ... everything arriving from the coasts of the Mediterranean ... used to be

[229] The only major banker of the 1770s period that is missing from chamber membership was John Gregson, though he was a probable member and a partner of Case who was a member; see Hughes, 1906, pp 108–10.
[230] See Baines 1852; Brooke, 1853; Williams, 1897, and sources in Table A.2.
[231] Gatty, 1882: Mugs 43, 44 etc; see also Boney, 1957.

consigned, and to whom every foreigner, if he could speak English, had a letter of introduction".[232] An analysis of slave traders by Inikori (1981) shows nine of the chamber members as leading slave traders by volume of shipping (Tarleton, Staniforth, the Hodgsons, Ingram, Leyland, Case, Nottingham, Earle), though Dawson, Boates and Davenport, by far the largest slave traders, do not appear to have been members. The chamber committee, therefore, was a general interest body across many major sectors, giving a broad representation of the main trading and commercial interests in the city, but it contained a disproportionate number of the major merchants, many of the major slave traders, and a near monopoly of Liverpool bankers. It thus can be judged as a body of the business elite, though it omitted some major businesses and included some more minor ones.

Fifth, compared with the composition of the city by sector, the chamber was more focused on merchants and banking, which are both proportionately strongly over-represented. Manufacturing is under-represented in the chamber, though less so when merchants who were also manufacturers are included.[233] The smaller representation of manu-facturers is typical of chambers until the late 19th century.

Trading markets

A further indicator of membership interests is analysis of the main trading markets of leading members. These can be identified with some confidence for 60 of the 65 known, and 20 of the probable members (Table 7). This shows the chamber members to be part of the strong inter-linkage of Liverpool with the Atlantic economy and the complex trade between Africa, America, the West Indies and Britain, and the Greenland fisheries with Europe. The majority of the chamber's members were in these trades. Only two were engaged primarily in European trade. Those traders who were involved in Europe were mainly in specialist trades: James (cattle), Corrie (corn), Earle (manu-factured exports), Hodgson (sugar), Leyland (meat), Manley and Ryan (wine). But for most of these Europe was only part of their business. The group of businesses primarily focused on the UK or Ireland were manufacturers, merchants (mainly of linen), warehousing and shipping packet services.

The chamber members were more focused on the long range Amer-ican, West Indies and African trade than the port's shipping as a whole. Comparison in 1790–1, for example, shows Liverpool trade through

---

[232] Boardman, 1871, p 13.
[233] See also Haggerty, 2002.

Table 7 Main trading markets of Liverpool chamber of commerce members in c1780

	Known (no)	Known (%)	Probable (no)	Probable (%)
America, including Greenland (mainly)	16	26.2	5	25.0
Africa (mainly)	5	8.2	4	20.0
West Indies (mainly)	3	4.9	1	5.0
America, and Africa and West Indies combined	20	32.8	6	30.0
Europe (mainly)	2	3.3	1	5.0
Europe and America and West Indies	11	18.0	-	-
UK/Ireland (mainly)	4	6.6	3	15.0

British vessels in tonnage was 17–18% to Africa and the West Indies, 9–14% to the Americas and Greenland, 19–26% to northern Europe (including France), 7–6% to southern Europe and the Mediterranean, and 36% fisheries and coasting.[234] This estimates the long-range trade as 45–58% of shipping, compared with the chamber's known members at 90% (although they were mostly in several markets). Since the long-range trades generally needed larger credits, this is another factor explaining the linkages of the banking and insurance businesses to this group of traders.

Slave trade

A major feature of Liverpool's trading structure was, of course, the slave trade. In Appendix Tables A.2 and A.3, slaving is noted where this is believed to have been a significant part of activity, though all the other Africa shippers and merchants (except Wallace who was opposed on grounds of religion) undoubtedly would have had at least some involvement. There were 31 (48%) of the known members, and 43% of the probable members with known trade interests. Another indicator of very strong involvement in the slave trade is membership of the Africa Company. After its reform in 1750, 'freemen' membership of the company was available for the fairly nominal payment of two guineas. In 1756, 92 (21.8%) of its membership was from Liverpool.[235]

---

[234] This quotes the in-trade and then the out-trade, respectively; from BL Add MS 38351, f.112: *List of British vessels at Liverpool trading with each country*; a further 250–260 vessels and 47–49,000 tons are excluded which were carried through foreign vessels.
[235] Count of first lists of freemen of Africa Company: TNA T70/1508.

The Liverpool records of freemen were kept in the Liverpool Africa Company Minute Book, which elected a chair and other officers.[236] Using these sources, 29% of the known chamber members, and 39% of the probables can be identified as freemen of the company, with some joining only in the 1790s (see Appendix Tables A.4 and A.5).

The slaving interest was thus a large interest of the chamber members; but it was only one major concern of a diversified membership. However, when slave trade abolition began to gain momentum, chiefly after the introduction of Dolben's Bill in 1788 to limit the carrying capacity of slave ships, it became a very divisive issue. A full analysis of the chamber members views is not possible, given the absence of records. But from the earlier discussion it is clear that the chamber had strong advocates on both sides of the question. Moreover, even among the slave traders there was strong diversity, as evident from "the want of unanimity" when the chamber proposed to fight a legal action related to the Jamaican slave tax in 1774–5. Thus, even then those involved in the trade were too diverse to agree on joint action.

Women

It is not surprising that all the known and probable chamber members were men. Few women could enter into business on their own account, particularly to become an entrepreneur engaged in a major business, or one that involved major credit or overseas trading. Almost all females in business in Liverpool at this time were small retailers, artisans or employees.[237] However, some opportunities arose mainly as a result of inheriting a business or capital on the death of a husband or relative. The advertisement for the Tontine Hotel (Bates) demonstrates awareness of appealing to both women and men, while the subscription library was already open to and used by many women.

There is one woman in Liverpool who was certainly in a commanding business position at this time: Sarah Clayton, the aunt of chamber member Thomas Case. She was one of the main proprietors of Sankey Navigation after 1754, ran her own flats carriage business, and was a leader in marketing St Helens coal in Liverpool operating under the name of Clayton, Case & Co. She was also politically active in support of the Tory cause and the Corporation: she was one of the supporters of John Tarleton senior's unsuccessful bid to become a Liverpool MP in 1767–8, and one of the few willing to subscribe to his cause. She was also active enough to be the only woman among 49 men attending a

---

[236] Committee Book of Africa Company of Liverpool: LRO 352 MD1.
[237] Haggerty, 2002, 2006.

political meeting for Tarleton, in May 1768.[238] Whilst the absence of a full membership list prevents us knowing whether she was a chamber member, she was recognised as a 'femme formidable' and was the sort of person who would be, even though her politics were conventional rather than reform minded. And she was one of the most strongly connected individuals with others who were members: both Nicholas Ashton and Thomas Case were partners in her business, who were brothers-in-law of each other; another of her partners was John Blackburne junior, the first chair of the committee of trade; and there were also strong interrelationships with the Nicholsons.[239]

Another possible female chamber member would have been the widow of David Tuohy, who was a probable chamber member and partner of chamber members Leyland, the Heywoods, Ingram, and probable members Parke and Speers. David Tuohy was a major merchant who died in 1788. It appears that his wife, and probably his daughter, continued some of his business activities.[240] If not actually a chamber member, the wife of Tuohy, as active business proprietor, would have been very close to the chamber's committee.

[238] LRO 920 TAR/3/11.
[239] Hughes, 1906, p 189; Nicholson, 1928; Barker, 1949, p 124; Barker and Harris, 1959.
[240] Haggerty, 2006, pp 221, 227–34; supplemented by IGI.

11
Business networks

Liverpool was one of the world's first major industrial cities, serving a large hinterland that was also rapidly developing. The businesses in the city and the region, like today's, relied on formal legal and informal structures so that their trade and exchanges with each other could be relied upon, and their marketing developed. This required a wide range of networks: for supply, for marketing, for credit and banking, and for broking, insurance, agency and shipping activities. Elsewhere, attention has been drawn to the importance of business networks and social/family relationships in how local economies of the 18th century were developing.[241] The Liverpool chamber appears to be strongly inter-related with many of the key business networks operating in the city at the time. There were Scottish, Irish, Cumberland, Yorkshire and other sources of kinship to some of these networks, relating to where some families originated; but some of the strongest ties were through religion, business structures and marriage.[242] This would have facilitated the chamber's formation, and helped to sustain it by encouraging the sharing of understanding and common interests. These networks of trust and obligation would be important underpinnings to developing a common platform for lobbying.

[241] See eg Schofield, 1964; Checkland, 1952, 1958; Morgan, 2000; Pearson and Richardson, 2001; Wilson and Popp, 2003a, 2003b.
[242] Eg Checkland, 1952, 1971; Pope, 1970; Haggerty, 2006.

Formal networks and partnerships

A complete analysis of the business networks of Liverpool's chamber members is not possible given the information available. But some important insights can be derived. One derives from the corporate form of the businesses involved. This period is before the time of limited liability companies, but it is widely recognised that quasi-corporate forms were nevertheless developed through trusts and common law partnerships (usually denoted: & Co, or Bros, Sons etc), in the same way that the chamber itself was established. Appendix Tables A.1 and A.2 list those where the evidence suggests that this corporate form was used. This is derived from trade directories, heavily supplemented from other sources.[243]

It is notable that 58 of the 65 known members of the chamber (89%), and 82% of the probable members, were using a partnership form of business in c1780. Only 11 were trading solely as individuals in their sole names, although, of the partnerships, many traded as both individuals and '& Co' for different business activities. This finding is perhaps not surprising for Liverpool, whose wide use of partnerships in this period has been recognised.[244] But it is much higher than for many other leading centres at this time, and demonstrates the wide development of formal economic structures that helped to underpin other relationships such as membership of a chamber.

Since partnerships were generally larger businesses than sole traders, their high proportion also echoes the conclusion that a significant proportion of the major Liverpool businesses were leading members of the chamber. Their size also interrelates with their form of trade, involving long sea voyages with significant capital tied up in shipping and commodity cargoes for long periods that had to be financed. This trade naturally lent itself to the need for co-operative activity, both to raise the necessary capital and to share risk. It also drew on the tradition of investing in ships, their cargoes, or their voyages in fractions. Liverpool is noted for the concentration of its ownership of shipping. Half of the vessels were owned by only one or two people, which is much higher than London, Bristol or other ports.[245] Hence co-operation through formal partnerships was widespread in Liverpool, and is reflected in its leading chamber members. In turn, this sharing of capital and risk naturally interlocked with the significant development of local

---

[243] Gore's directory for 1781 is significantly larger in its listings of individuals not in major trades, and its coverage of partnerships is more limited; Baine's Northern Directory of 1781 gives smaller but fuller supplementary coverage of partnership links; but the main source is more detailed analysis of records reported in the sources listed in Tables A.2 and A.3.

[244] Checkland, 1952; Pope, 1970, 2007; Belchem, 1992; Pearson and Richardson, 2001; Haggerty, 2006.

[245] Craig and Jarvis, 1967, Tables 24 and 25.

banking and insurance, as represented by the wide banking and insurance interests of the merchants, and their high representation among the members of the chamber.

Information on the pattern of partnership links among the chamber's committee can only be partial, given the records available. But even with the constraints, it is clear that many of the chamber's committee were closely connected with each other, to an extent that went beyond a general interest in the trade of Liverpool: many were also lenders, borrowers, joint investors, customers or suppliers to each other. Edgar Corrie had been an apprentice to John Dobson; John Bolton to Rawlinson and Chorley (and was sent by Chorley to the West Indies); Francis Ingram to the Heywoods, as had Matthew Nicholson; Thomas Lake to Thomas Smythe; and Benjamin Heywood to James Crosbie; Thomas Staniforth to Charles Goore. John Walker's apprenticeship to his father was completed under John Dobson and Dalterra & Co after his father's death in 1769. John Gore, who advertised the chamber's initial meeting, and ran a major newspaper, was assisted by the Nicholson family in establishing his business in the 1760s.[246] Of the probable chamber members, Thomas Parke was the most interconnected (with Ingram, Carruthers, Denison, the Heywoods, Speers, and later with Tuohy and Gregson).

Apprenticeship, which often depended on family connections, frequently matured into subsequent partnership. The full list of major known partner links is recorded in Appendix Tables A.2 and A.3. Some of the most significant linked Dobson, Robert Nicholson, Thomas Hodgson and others as partners in various ventures. William Wallace, John Chorley and the Rawlinsons were business partners. The Ashton and Case families were closely interlinked in joint ventures to develop the coal and salt at St Helens and Wigan and to open the Sankey canal. Another link was through the Liverpool Fire Insurance office established in February 1777, where Gill Slater, Richard Heywood, John Tarleton, Thomas Case, BA Heywood, Benjamin Heywood, Thomas Tarleton and Thomas Parke were the initial directors.[247] All are known or probable chamber committee members. Even as late as 1802, the Liverpool St George's Fire Office had two of its six trustees from the chamber.[248] As often noted,[249] Liverpool businesses were strongly interconnected, forming and dissolving partnerships frequently, as needed, and most

---

[246] Register of Freeman records; see also Pope, 1970, vol. 2; Matthews, 1941; Chandler, 1964; Checkland, 1971.

[247] Williamsons Advertiser, 28 February 1777; Baines, 1852, p 453; see also Pearson and Richardson, 2001.

[248] Thomas Leyland, John Gregson, and Heywood descendant Arthur; Baines, 1852, p 510.

[249] Checkland, 1952; Belchem, 1992; Pope, 1970, vol. 2, p 298 ff., Pope, 2007.

Matthew Nicholson, 1746-1819   Richard Heywood, 1751-1800

major businesses were very entrepreneurial, having a wide range of other local business involvements. The chamber seems to have contained a leading group of these interconnected businesses.

The formal basis of co-operation within the Liverpool business networks also reinforces the interpretation of the chamber as a relatively general representative body. Many of the leading members were not only business partners with each other, through their direct family and outside it, but also business partners with others who are not known as members of the chamber. In addition, the de facto leadership of the chamber exercised by these leading businesses was a clear signal to others: it should have stimulated other businesses to want to become members or give support. Loyalty to a place and the co-ordination of a unity of voice for the chamber, therefore, could more easily develop if there was already a loyalty to each other. It was probably more a facilitative rather than a necessary or a sufficient condition, since some important businesses and others down the credit chain do not appear to have become members, but economic and other obligations would have been critically important drivers for trying to achieve a wide and expanding membership.

Social and relational networks

Economic networks were only part of the connectivity of the Liverpool chamber: the members were also socially connected. Again, a full analysis is impossible given the incompleteness of sources, but the available evidence (summarised in Appendix Tables A.4 and A.5) confirms that there were many important linkages between the leading members through the most important social and informal networks of the time.

Societies

Perhaps most important to link some of the early core chamber members was 'The Unanimous Society', an important elite coffee, drinking and social club established in 1753 and lasting until 1778, to which many of the leading chamber members belonged. Alexander Nottingham, Thomas Case, and George Venables were presidents in some years, John Chorley a secretary. Nine chamber members were also society members. It attracted "gentlemen of the first families of the town".[250] The demise of the Society in 1778 may have been a result of the success of the chamber, which replaced it, or dissent over politics and America which forced members to take sides (as investigated further below). An earlier, and even more elitist group was an 'Ugly Face Society' for which records survive for 1743–57. Three of the approximately 20 Ugly Face members were also chamber members (John Kennion, Benjamin Heywood and Thomas Hodgson), but there were links to others through John Tarleton senior and Robert Hesketh. This was another drinking and social group who enjoyed writing lurid descriptions of how ugly each member was.[251] The fact that few probable chamber members were members of these societies confirms the chamber's committee as part of an elite among the businesses.

Another social network, but with a more popular and semi-serious political intent, was the 'Sefton (or Sephton) Mock Corporation', which covered 1753–1829. This was a large-scale organisation whose purpose was to stage mock elections to ridicule the Corporation's, as well as holding huge dinners and social events. Between 60–75% of its members were merchants and traders, but it was not exclusive, having a membership of several hundred, some of whom came from Manchester, Birmingham, Kendal, or further afield. Many of the chamber members were members of this society: 30 (46%) of the chamber known, and nine (39%) of the chamber probable, members were members of the Sefton Mock Corporation. James Carruthers and John Dobson were joint 'mayors' of it in 1767–8, Thomas Foxcroft in 1762–3, and probable chamber member Anthony Grayson in 1756–7. A particularly large number of chamber members joined the Mock Corporation in 1771–74 (about 30% of the chamber members that joined); but after 1774 no known or probable chamber members joined.[252] This pattern is indicative of a symmetry between the Sefton Mock Corporation and the chamber members' concerns about the real Corporation, and indigna-

---

[250] LRO 367 UNA/1; see also Brooke, 1853, pp 290–8; Boardman, 1871.
[251] LRO UGL 1/1.
[252] Analysis of the minutes and joining list: LRO 367 SEF 1 and 2; see also Horley, 1881; Saxton, 1949; Haggerty, 2006, p 133.

tion with the behaviour of John Parr, John Sparling and his colleagues. It may have allowed them to let off steam, and perhaps it offered the milieu for the concept of a chamber to form in people's minds, especially during the period when Carruthers and Dobson were 'mayors'. After 1774, the fact that no new chamber members were recruited to the Mock Corporation suggests that the chamber now fulfilled some of the needs for business leaders to marshal their political objectives.

The other indicator of the critical importance of social networking to the chamber members is the brief concluding comments of the 1777 *Abstract*, as noted earlier, to have a meeting room for the chamber. This was a primary function of most of the other early chambers, and must have been a stimulus for the four chamber members to initiate the Bates Hotel Tontine in 1783. Moreover, 20 (43%) of the chamber's known and three (18%) of the probable membership still alive or active at the time became founding members of the Liverpool Athenaeum when it was launched in 1797 (Appendix Tables A.4 and A.5). The chamber was thus closely linked to other prominent social networks.

Benevolent, cultural and improvement bodies

Chamber members were also leading members, with others, of other major institutions. Again there are many examples, but especially noteworthy we find in 1774 that Chorley, Dobson, Nottingham and Chaffers were Commissioners of the Docks; Case, Slater, Brooks, Dobson and Benjamin Heywood were Commissioners of the Watch; and Brooks and Slater members of the Pilots Committee.[253] Falkner, Earle, Leyland and Staniforth were leading members of the 'Hundred of West Derby Agricultural (Improvement) Society'.[254] The Dispensary, established in 1778, had Joseph Brooks as treasurer, Nicholas Ashton as president, and 14 of the chamber members among the 102 initial subscribers.[255] Staniforth was president, and Brooks, Nottingham, Slater and Dobson were committee members for the Seamen's Hospital in 1774.

They were also an active group in other cultural bodies in the city. Thomas Staniforth was president of the Music Hall, forerunner of the Philharmonic Society,[256] to which at least six other chamber members as well as members of the committee on trade acted as stewards for concerts.[257] Nicholas Ashton was president of a Society for Promoting

---

[253] Gore's Directory, 1774.

[254] LRO 630 WES.

[255] Brooke, 1853, pp 360–4; the chamber subscribers were Ashton, Brooks, Corrie, Falkner, A and B Heywood, Kennion, Manley, Mears, Rathbone, Staniforth, Wagner, Watt, Wallace.

[256] Quoted in Hext, 1965, p 8.

[257] Nicholas Ashton, Joseph Birch, John Blackburne jun, Thomas Earle, Edward Falkner, John Gregson, Benjamin Arthur Heywood, John Lightbody, William Roe, Gill Slater, Thomas Staniforth, Thomas Tarleton, and Richard Walker; quoted from local newspapers by Pope, 1970, vol. 2, p 458.

Painting in the 1780s.[258] The Liverpool Subscription Library (later called the Lyceum Library after moving in 1803), founded in 1758, had most of the chamber members as subscribers (71% of known and 35% of probable). The Committee of the Library was also extensively populated by chamber members (see Appendix Tables A.4 and A.5), and were among its initial subscribers. This library was an interesting innovation in itself, the first such library in England (though there was an earlier one in Scotland), copied in many other industrial towns over the 1760s and 1770s, and open to women as well as men. It was a major source of information and provided a meeting/reading and coffee room (68 by 48 feet), mainly for the business community, but apart from a collection of commercial material most of its holdings were on travel, poetry, literature, American commentaries, history, farmers guides, science, and a range of journals.[259] It was to some extent superseded by the Athenaeum when this was established in 1797, and many of the surviving chamber members joined.

The overlapping memberships of these bodies is illustrated in Figure 2, drawn from the Appendix Tables. The more populist Library and Sefton Corporation can be distinguished from the more elitist Unanimous Society. The Athenaeum cut across these groups, with few members in common with the Unanimous Society. If we use the overlappings as a guide to connectivity, then George Venables appears as the most connected (a member of all four bodies), followed by Ashton, Caruthers, Dunbar, E Falkner, Hodgson senior, Foxcroft, Kent and Parke. These individuals also form an important part of the core of the chamber committee, seven of them being committee members for at least eight years. Hence, social connections were supportive of the chamber's own networks.

Family and friends

Many of the chamber members were also strongly socially engaged with each other. The Rathbone family histories and records show extensive informal social networking and active dining among many of the chamber circle and many other regional and national figures.[260] For example, Matthew Nicholson, Robert Bent and William Wallace were close contacts of the Rathbones and Croppers.[261] Thomas Staniforth's letterbooks and papers show that he and his wife were regularly dining

---

[258] Brooke, 1853, p 534.

[259] Analysis of Library membership, catalogue and purchases: LRO 027 LYC 1/1/1, 1/1/2 and 3/1; see also Troughton, 1810, pp 343–4.

[260] Rathbone, 1913, pp 111–3.

[261] Letters from William Rathbone to Benson Rathbone jun 7 August and 17 November 1786: RP.II.1.1–3: Liverpool University Library.

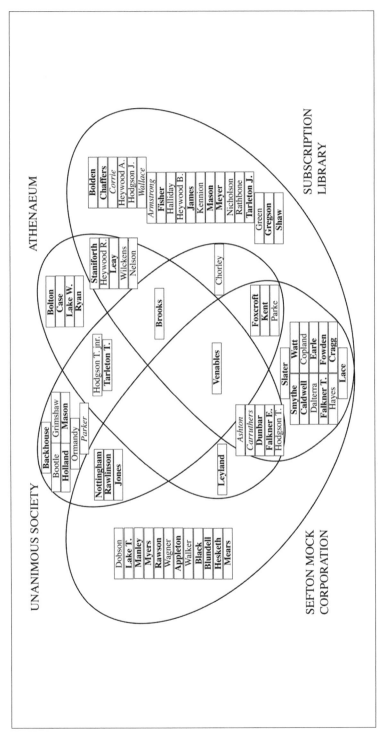

Figure 2 The overlapping membership of the main Liverpool societies and institutions 1770–1800; Anglicans shown in bold, dissenters shown without emphasis; uncertain or changed religion in italics

with Slater, Rawlinson and other chamber members. Staniforth, Brooks junior, and Chaffers in 1777 and 1780 travelled to London together on business matters. Staniforth went fishing in Cumberland and to the Keswick Regatta 14–24 August 1779 with Edward Chaffers; and again in 1780.[262] Jonathan Blundell (probable member) and the Heywoods were close friends.[263] Gill Slater and Joseph Brooks junior were respectively captain and lieutenant of a volunteer corps raised in September 1782 which involved a wide range of other volunteers from inside and outside the chamber, receiving their colours in February 1783 from the King and the wife of Henry Rawlinson (cousin of chamber member T H Rawlinson).[264]

Informal social networks also brought formal obligations. When Thomas Staniforth's "honest friend" Alexander Nottingham died on 7 March 1781, the bearers were Thomas Tarleton, Thomas Staniforth, Joseph Brooks junior, Thomas Ryan, Thomas Hodgson and two others not on the chamber committee. Edward Chaffers and Staniforth were the official mourners at the funeral of Mr Taylor on 27 September 1780.[265] At James Carver's funeral on 8 January 1786, Joseph Brooks junior, Caldwell, Dunbar, Halliday, Slater and Staniforth were bearers.

There were also many marriages and other kinship links between the chamber members. For example, Joseph Brooks' (senior) sister was married to John Ashton, father of Nicholas Ashton; and he was also uncle to Joseph Brooks junior. Thomas Staniforth, after being apprenticed to Charles Goore, a prominent slave trader, married his only daughter. Staniforth helped Thomas Tarleton at Fleet Prison, 11 August 1778. Samuel Staniforth, Thomas's brother, married into the Case and Bolton families. Thomas Case was married to the sister of Nicholas Ashton,[266] while Ashton's eldest son married Elizabeth Earle, granddaughter of William. Richard Heywood, son of Arthur, was married to William Earle's daughter Mary.[267] John Chorley married Sarah Rawlinson, a relation of another chamber member.[268] Hugh Henry Leigh was interrelated with the Cases and Claytons, and the Claytons also provided a family connection to the Ashtons. Edward Falkner was married to Thomas Tarleton's daughter Bridget.[269] John Tarleton and Arthur Heywood were married to the sisters Penelope and Hannah Milnes,

[262] LRO STI 1/3/1–4.
[263] Pope, 1970, vol. 2, p 465.
[264] Brooke, 1853, pp 372–3: Henry Rawlinson was MP for Liverpool 1780–4; Thorne, History of Parliament gives the family relationships.
[265] A selection of many comments in Thomas Staniforth's letterbooks, memorandum books and notebooks for 1776–93: LRO STI 1/3/1–4; STI 1/2/1–3; STI 1/4/1; see also Aspinall, 1852.
[266] Hughes, 1906; Barker and Harris, 1959, p 51; Pope, 1970, vol. 2.
[267] Earle, 1890, p 47; Hughes, 1906, p 96.
[268] Lancaster Congregational Chapel records: TNA RG 6.
[269] Brooke, 1853, p 376.

respectively, both daughters receiving settlements in their father's will (Richard Milnes), as well as undertaking pre-nuptial settlements.[270] Both married within a month of each other in 1750. The Heywoods, Tarletons, Milnes and Stephen Hayes were also all interrelated with the Pemberton family,[271] all using the Pemberton name for some of their offspring. For Arthur Heywood this was through a first marriage to Elizabeth, daughter of Samuel Ogden of Mossley Hill, in 1739 (she died in 1748), from whom he inherited a large fortune from her grandfather John Pemberton. His brother Benjamin Heywood was married to another Ogden who was the joint heiress of John Pemberton. This produced a complex set of family and business interrelationships.[272] Similarly, Charles Caldwell was married to another Heywood family member, Elizabeth.[273]

The Nicholsons were a wide merchant family in their own right, with business partnerships and marriages with John Dobson, the Hodgsons, Croppers, Claytons and others. They were intimates of Percival at the Warrington Academy, and Thomas Butterworth Bayley in Manchester. The known chamber member Matthew Nicholson's father Robert had married Arabella Cropper, through whom he became related to the Pembertons and Heywoods (as well as the Jones bankers in Manchester). He became the chief cashier of the Heywoods' bank when it opened in Manchester in 1788, remaining in that position until his retirement in 1832.[274] Probable member William Ormandy was married to another Cropper. Thus the Croppers, Claytons, Goores and Pembertons appear to be a set of important connecting family ties between chamber members, though they are now known as members themselves.

It is difficult to render all these connections into a single representation, but Figure 3 illustrates in the three ellipses the core trading structure of Liverpool merchants: membership of the Africa Company, those involved with the slave trade, and those whose flags were used to denote them as major merchants in contemporary pottery. Some of the highly connected individuals outside this trade are also shown. This shows the tight connectivity of these groups, but also illustrates how slaving brought in a wide range of smaller merchants in addition to the larger concerns. It also demonstrates how the Africa Company was no longer the only structure for the slavers: many of the largest slavers

---

[270] Marriage articles of Penelope Milnes and John Tarleton, 18 March 1750; CM/1109; prenuptial agreement of Hannah Milnes and Arthur Heywood, 23 April 1750, CM/1503 [Crewe Muniments: Sheffield Archives].

[271] Articles of agreement on Richard Milnes' will, 24 February 1755; CM/150 and CM/1506 [Crewe Muniments].

[272] Ormerod, 1952.

[273] From IGI.

[274] Nicholson, 1928, pp 64–5; 132–5; Ormerod, 1952.

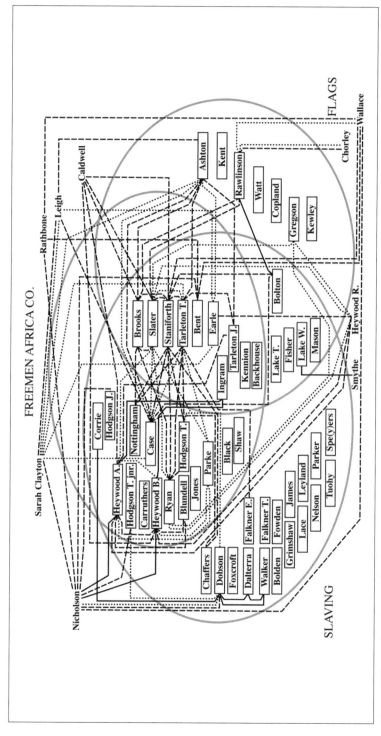

Figure 3 The overlapping membership of Africa Company, slaving and major businesses (as indicated by their flags shown on contemporary pottery), and their interconnection through apprenticeships (solid lines), partnerships (dotted lines), and family/marriage ties (dashed lines)

were not members. Moreover, slaving was not the only trade that provided scope to be a large merchant: seven of the largest merchant businesses had little or no involvement, though some had plantation interests.

Figure 3 also attempts to show apprenticeship, business partnership, and friendship/family/marriage links. The intention is to highlight the most connected individuals through the widest range of the known ties. Within the Africa Company, slaving and large businesses, the core group numbers ten. Of these Slater, Staniforth, Thomas Tarleton, Ingram and Brooks were the most connected, both through partnerships and marriage ties. Outside this group Nottingham, Case, Benjamin and Arthur Heywood, Hodgson senior, Ryan, Dobson, Ashton and Rawlinson were the most connected, but through apprenticeships as well as marriage and partnership links. In addition, several others had numerous ties with the core group, but were not Africa traders or slavers: particularly Wallace, Richard Heywood, Caldwell, Sarah Clayton, and especially Nicholson, being most important. It is noteworthy that almost all of these individuals were core chamber members, elected to the committee for at least eight years. However, Sarah Clayton, though not a known chamber member, stands out as an individual with many avenues of influence. The figure thus brings out how the chamber was focused on links between the core trading interests of the city, but also shows the networks linking the main businesses that were not slave traders.

Comparing these focal individuals with the most connected through societies (Figure 2) shows overlaps, but also contrasts. Although the incomplete nature of the information constrains conclusions, generally the social networks were wider ranging than the trading and partnership/family ties. But it was possible to have high connectivity through either group of ties. Perhaps the most connected individual of all across business, family and social structures was Slater; hence, it is not surprising that he became an early chamber chair. Dobson, the first chair, owed his connectivity largely to apprenticeship ties; his business (corn dealing) was less connected to the main Liverpool merchant structures in the Africa trade (though he was also involved). But his role as first chair may thus have derived as much from the force of his personality and his leadership against the Corporation as his wider connectivity in the city. It was his anger that helped to catalyse others; but it was Slater who seems to have been able to guide the chamber forwards over most of its early years, probably helped by the breadth of his networks.

Religious networks and ties

Religion was very important in this period. First, it provided another forum for networking and basis for mutual trust; and additional and sometimes a primary basis for developing social and marriage ties. It was certainly a critical element in bringing together some businesses; eg the Earles and Heywoods, leading to the Earles becoming leading figures in Heywoods' bank in later years (especially after the 1830s).[275] Second, being a dissenter or Catholic strictly meant exclusion from government, Corporation and other formal positions, as a result of the Corporation and Test Acts. In practice, these restrictions were often insignificant if an individual did not draw attention to their beliefs; and in Liverpool there is said to have been a high degree of tolerance at this time.[276] But the restrictions would have increased support for initiatives that sought reform.

For the dissenters, collective acts of reading and commentary on texts and education were often strong stimuli to political engagement, encouraged by the preachers who were often radical advocates of reform in a period in which the dissenting chapels were debating John Wilkes' proposals, Thomas Paine's 1786 *Rights of Man* and the French Revolution of 1789. For the Anglicans, religion was part of the establishment, with which leading families would wish to become deeply engaged. Religion was thus part of a more general political divide between reform and conservatism, which interrelated with attitudes to institutions such as the Corporation. Religion was thus a potential divide between those who sought reform or acquiesced in a corrupt electoral process that maintained the aristocracy in power. Religion was also beginning to become an important divide in attitudes to the slave trade, with the Quakers becoming totally opposed and several other dissenting groups becoming more critical.

Appendix Tables A.4 and A.5 show the religious allegiances of the chamber members, as far as these can be traced. In assessing this table it must be borne in mind that this is a snapshot: people may have changed their beliefs over time (as Nicholas Ashton seems to have done), and for all denominations, then as now, affiliation might be nominal. Of those where their religion can be definitely identified, among the known members a maximum of 40% were dissenters (including Catholics), and a maximum of 65% Anglicans (with the Presbyterians and Unitarians being most prominent, though the Rathbones were Quakers, until William was expelled). For the probable members,

---

[275] Chandler, 1964, pp 175–6 and ff.
[276] See eg Checkland, 1952; Bradley, 1990.

the proportion of dissenters is lower: a maximum of 21.7%, and a maximum of 82.6% Anglicans. The dissenters were thus a very substantial proportion of the chamber's membership, particularly of the leadership group. The dissenter proportion is also much higher than the general Liverpool population, which was no more than 10% in the 1770s.[277]

Among the dissenter members, some were notably radical. William Rathbone IV, uncle of Joseph (the chamber member) and 'éminence grise' of the family at this time, was strongly aligned with the Irish Friends, whose theology was too radical for many English Quakers; indeed, William was denounced for his role in Ireland, disowned by the Friends in 1805, became a Unitarian, and was buried in the non-Quaker part of the burial ground in 1809.[278]

The Heywoods were prominent Unitarians and active as trustees of the Warrington Academy, with Arthur Heywood its treasurer. This academy was a college for training young men for the dissenter clergy and other professional walks of life. It inculcated a sense of duty to community and doing good works. It had natural affinities to the concept of a chamber of commerce that sought to represent a general local community interest. It was also a source of linkage between the first president of the Manchester chamber, Thomas Butterworth Bayley, other Manchester chamber interests, and several Liverpool chamber members, notably the Heywoods and the first chair John Dobson.[279] Samuel Green's religion is uncertain, because of the commonness of his name, but it is probable that he was a dissenter, since dissenter births best fit his known birth year, and a Mr S Green donated the bell to the Octagon chapel in 1762.[280]

The high proportion of dissenters might be partly accounted for by their greater sympathy with, or understanding of, the chamber idea, since most chapels required active assent to become 'members'. Hence a commitment might mean more to dissenters, treated as a vow of obligation to do something. Indeed, dissenters nationally were often politically more active and, in Liverpool, the dissenters were often the most politically most active of the merchants.[281] Political activism is assessed further below in the context of petitioning.

But whatever the different levels of activism of dissenters and Anglicans, it would be wrong to see the chamber as a direct offshoot of

---

[277] Dissenting congregations numbered about 1,500–2,000 in the 1770s for Liverpool and Toxteth Park (Thompson list, BL Add Ms. 32057); see also Evans, 1887; Roberts, 1909; Bradley, 1990, pp 274–5.
[278] Biographical entry in Milligan, 2007.
[279] See Fox Bourne, 1886, pp 298–330; Turner, 1957.
[280] Nightingale, 1893, pp 128–38.
[281] Evans, 1887; Roberts, 1909; Bradley, 1990.

dissenter thought and a specific form of community commitment. While the dissenters were disproportionately represented, the chamber members came from all religious camps. Also, dissenters did not have a monopoly on community or altruism; many Anglicans were similarly supportive of local initiatives and community, but differed about what community meant, and their degree of acceptance of hierarchy and reverence for custom.

Thus the chamber appears to reflect the relatively religiously relaxed atmosphere of Liverpool at this time, where many major public activities crossed the religious divides.[282] This included societies, where the cross-sectarian membership of the Unanimous and Sefton societies, Athenaeum and Subscription Library by chamber members is evident in Figure 2. It is also demonstrated by a subscription initiative to establish Sunday schools in November 1784. This might be expected to show strong division along religious lines. But, among the 59 subscribers to the initiative, 13–15 were chamber members, of whom two were dissenters or Catholic.[283] Other cross-sectarian subscriptions were normal for other good causes (as seen in many of the subscription lists in the newspapers, and the subscriptions for books and activities of the chapels).[284] Indeed, the parish Vestry, while dominated by Anglicans for all the major parish posts, nevertheless had some dissenter members (notably Benjamin Heywood) for some of its major activities (the Commissioners of the Watch, Commissioners of the Workhouse).

These cross-sectarian initiatives, and the heavy involvement of the Anglicans and a few dissenter chamber members in reform of the Vestry, throws in some doubt Checkland's interpretation of the economic attitudes of Liverpool in this period. He saw the Corporation and the established church as aligned to economic protectionism, and dissenters working from outside to challenge slavery and established mercantilist positions.[285]

Certainly the business community in the chamber of commerce was associated with diverse religious points of view. Its leading members were certainly reform minded, but some of its Anglicans were as reform minded in the efforts to improve the established church Vestry as any

---

[282] Analysis of religious influences on general election voting in Liverpool, for example, fails to find any statistically significant differences between the groups, and small sample sizes make all these tables unreliable: reanalysis of Tables 8.6 and 8.7 in Bradley 1990.

[283] Brooke, 1853, pp 379–382; the chamber members were Brooks, Lace, Nelson, Rawson, Slater, Chaffers, Benjamin A Heywood, Kent, Wallace, Watt, Falkner, Lake, Meyer; and probable members Blundell and Hesketh.

[284] See eg subscription lists in Roberts, 1909.

[285] Checkland, 1952, especially pp 61–7. This has been echoed in some more recent commentary, where Bradley has argued that the dissenters were a critical force associated with reform movements generally, and supporters of the rights of the American colonies in particular; Bradley, 1986, 1990.

of the dissenters. The chamber contained both pro- and anti-slave trade abolitionists, and the dissenters were also split on the issue: 44% of chamber dissenters were slave traders in 1780, and 62.5% of chamber Anglicans (of known and probable members). Overall the chamber appears to have sought to bind the different leading groups into general initiatives for change, of which the chamber itself was one key part. Checkland's interpretation of the city's economic attitudes seems to have been over-influenced by the attitudes of the Corporation (and its Committee of Trade). The re-discovery of the chamber's lost history thus offers some interesting new light on personal alignments that suggests that religion was an important feature that underlay social and economic networks rather than one that inexorably divided political or other viewpoints.[286] This interpretation can be taken further by analysis of petitioning.

---

[286] This is a conclusion also drawn by Haggerty, 2006, pp 135–9, using different evidence.

12
Political activism and alignment

Personal alignment also underpins the political networks of chamber members. Such networks were critical aspects of how the chamber related to other national and local forces of representation, and hence how far its voice and lobbies found support both in the wider community and within established political structures. The political position of chamber members is also an important test of how they saw their 'interest' compared with that of the Corporation, and hence allows further assessment of the proximate forces that led to the chamber's establishment.

At this time, the key political power lay with the King and court, parliament, and the local corporations. In one sense, the Liverpool chamber appears to have been well connected to these structures. The evidence of its lobbies, discussed above, shows the chamber able to use the established traditional routes of influence through MPs. In each case, the chamber developed a case or memorial/petition which was then sent to ministers or administrators through the local MPs.[287] This was part of the standard practice of petitioning by business and other interests in the period.[288] The petitioning sometimes worked with the Corporation, jointly or through separate petitions, and sometimes against it, as in 1790 over free and open ports.

[287] See Bennett, 2011 for analysis of the issues lobbied.
[288] See eg Brewer, 1989.

The Corporation was a self-electing body, independent of the government. In practice, however, major corporations like Liverpool's were subject to considerable attention by government, chiefly because the freemen were electors of MPs. Before most general elections, therefore, considerable numbers of new freemen were created in the hope of influencing the outcome. Procuring freemen who were potentially beholden to government was a major objective. This included officers of Customs and Excise, those dependent on government contracting, and those dependent on local sympathisers to the government. Customs officers were not removed from the electorate until 1782, but efforts had been made to remove them in 1770, 1780 and 1781.[289] Benjamin Heywood's specific annotation in his *Curious Papers* of those who were Customs, Excise and Common Councillors signing the coercion petition in 1775, shows they were recognised as one of many sources of government influence in the city. Heywood identified 21 members of the Common Council and 22 employed by Customs and Excise, amounting to 9% of the total of 471 signatures.[290]

General elections

Some of the chamber members were closely connected with the election of MPs. Before the foundation of the chamber, there had been a considerable electoral rumpus around the 1761 election of William Meredith, who later became a strong chamber supporter. This was seen as a strong attack on the Tarleton and Corporation interest at the time. William Ingram, father of chamber committee member Francis, was a principal backer of Meredith, who was chaired to Ingram's house after the election declaration in 1761.[291] Similarly in 1774, Thomas Staniforth hosted and paid for the celebratory dinner when Meredith was re-elected.[292] Arthur Heywood chaired and paid for Banastre Tarleton's election celebration dinner in 1791. Gill Slater and Richard Kent were deputies for Richard Pennant MP at the Bucks Society in 1768.[293]

The chamber members were clearly politically engaged at the most prominent local level in seeking to obtain what they considered to be more sympathetic representation locally than existing Corporation interests. Thus, on Banastre Tarleton's election, the invitation to dinner from Arthur Heywood was to "supporters of independent interest in Liverpool".[294] Banastre, brother of John, Thomas and Clayton, was an

[289] Kemp, 1953, p 262.
[290] Heywood Papers; the Corporation petition is a cutting from the London Chronicle, 6 October 1775; see further discussion below.
[291] Hughes, 1906, p 132.
[292] Williamsons Advertiser, 19 March 1774.
[293] Liverpool Chronicle, 27 February 1768.
[294] Williamsons Advertiser, 27 June 1791.

independent in parliament, usually voting with the opposition. The political engagement by the chamber members was also strongly inter-linked with national machinations in the 1760–80 period, chiefly related to the Rockingham party, for which Meredith and Banastre were the primary conduits.[295]

Freemen

A further issue is how far the chamber members were outsiders to the electoral process. Clearly some individuals were active in promoting alternative MPs for the city. But was their more general action to form a chamber related to a sense of exclusion from the Corporation and wider political life of the country? In terms of freemen there is little case to view the chamber as made up of those that were excluded: 39 (60%) of the chamber, known members, and nine (39%) of the probable chamber members were freemen, and almost all of these had achieved their freedom by 1774 when the chamber was established. The chamber members were probably not, therefore, explicitly seeking a different electoral franchise, and indeed most exercised their right to vote in the contested elections. Indeed, some members, particularly the Heywoods, Ingrams, Staniforths and Gregsons, were very actively involved in supporting particular candidates.

But the chamber members were not part of the true insiders forming the Common Council. This was the executive decision-making body of the Corporation, and it was their activities that were the concern of the chamber: the level of the trade duty, disputes over legal quays, apparent effrontery over Sparling's land, and the local point of view voiced over government regulations and policies (corn, tobacco, free trade with Ireland and the West Indies, and treatment of the American colonies). Only one of the probable chamber members had been a member of the Common Council by 1774 (Jonathan Blundell). The collective political concern was therefore not radical electoral changes, as espoused by many dissenting ministers and other radicals (and perhaps by a few members), but the exclusion of their interest from the key part of the system. The chamber was thus made up of the reform minded seeking entrées, rather than radicals.

Similarly, it is not easy to see the conflicts between chamber and Corporation just in terms of differences between specific trades. While the Corporation was certainly very focused on smaller businesses and the Africa trade,[296] the chamber also contained a large proportion of

---

[295] Investigated fully in Bennett, 2011, Chapter 4.
[296] Sanderson, 1977, p 66 states that over half of the Corporation's council in 1750 were freemen of the Africa Company; in 1787, 37 of the 41 councillors were owners of slave ships; in 1797 it was 34 of 38; see also Drescher, 1986; Longmore, 2007.

traders in these same markets. Analysis of the Corporation's committee of trade in terms of business markets and organisation closely parallels the chamber's known and probable members. They were both predominantly in large diversified partnership businesses, using partnership structures, and in similar markets. It is not true in the 1770s and 1780s, as claimed by Power for earlier years, that the Council was composed of the wealthiest.[297] There were now many others who were wealthy who were excluded from the Council and sought to gain a like influence. We have to see the tussle, therefore, not in terms of business interests, but in terms of conflicting networks of personality and power, as well as a different vision of business governance, seeking a broader unity of the major traders' interests: a group wrestling for voice with a Common Council that was perceived as impervious to their concerns.

Petitions

The chamber members were also part of a general movement to develop new voices directly to government through petitions. This was a traditional means of drawing attention to concerns and grievances, and seeking reformed legislation. The period running up to the chamber's establishment and the years immediately following was one of the most active and factional. These petitions did not generally emanate from the chamber itself, which the *Abstract* shows used the traditional route of sending memorials or 'cases' to government through its MPs, just as the Corporation did.

Petitions offered a more direct statement of concern and allowed a wider population than the chamber or the Corporation to become involved. They were inevitably more a statement of popular feelings. The petitions we are concerned with are those on economic issues signed by the "merchants, traders and inhabitants of Liverpool", or using some similar title. The extent of involvement of the chamber members with these petitions allows assessment of them as political actors, and how they related to political positions held in the wider local community.

Of the general petitions touching on business interests sent from Liverpool over this period (as distinct from narrow actions by the chamber itself or the Corporation), nine are selected that provide valuable insights into the political positions held by the chamber members:[298]

---

[297] Power, 1997, p 311.
[298] These petitions are held as follows: 1. TNA CO5/1330; 2. TNA T1/443/47; 3. TNA PRO 30/8/48, f. 183; 4. TNA T1/454/99–102; 5. TNA HO55/4/3; 6. TNA T1/498/182–3; 7. for the county of Lancaster, but listed separately for Liverpool, John Rylands Library, Manchester, published by C Wheeler, Eighteenth Century Online, with the original at TNA HO55/9/3; 8. TNA HO55/28/20; 9. LRO: MD 126.

1   Calling for suppression of paper money in Virginia in 1762.
2   Calling for repeal of the Stamp Act in 1765.
3   Thanking local MP William Meredith for his support in repeal of the Stamp Act 1766.
4   Seeking to extend the shipping lawful quays to include the South Dock and pier 1766.
5   Supporting John Wilkes and criticising the government over annulling the Middlesex election in 1769.
6   Supporting renewal of the Free Ports at Jamaica and Dominica for import and export in 1773.
7   In favour of peace and concessions in America in 1775.
8   In favour of coercion and the war in America in 1775.
9   Calling for the suppression of unnecessary offices in 1780.

These cover a period from well before the establishment of the chamber, through to the difficult period of international trade following the onset of war in America. The 1780 petition covers the later political issue of offices associated with resisting a general movement against government corruption. Using this long period permits analysis of how far the chamber's members were already deeply politically involved before the chamber was established, how that involvement evolved once the chamber existed, and how the chamber's involvement related to that of the Corporation (where comparison is made against the petitioning involvement of the Corporation's committee of trade). The relevance of these petitions is that, first, (except for Wilkes) they are on similar business and trade topics to the central lobbying activities of the chamber; and, second, they provide a wider listing of the business people who were at least marginally politically active – although signing a petition, of course, has no subscription cost and involves fairly nominal effort compared with active involvement in a chamber.

The importance of petitions over this period, and particularly with respect to American interests, has been widely recognised.[299] From the 1760s, there was large-scale petitioning on radical concerns, religion, and electoral reform, as well as covering trade. These could be very divisive, with local interests sending petitions for and against a particular position. In 1775, petitions regarding America were particularly divisive, with five of the 11 petitioning counties divided, and most of the major petitioning boroughs and towns also divided, including Liverpool; overall, there were about 26 peace petitions and 126 in favour of the American war, although the number of signatures was more equal

---

[299] See Muir, 1907, p 217–9; Bargar, 1956; Olson, 1973, 1979; Thomas, 1991; Bradley, 1986, 1990; Civin 2003.

between the two.[300] Several were massive indicators of public opinion; those for Wilkes and on America had 40,000 – 60,000 signatures nationally, as large as any vote in a general election. Others, like the Liverpool legal quays, and Free Ports, were specialised and only sought to engage sufficient leading local individuals to demonstrate the weight and respectability of the case being made. These petitions were more like memorials. The Stamp Act petitions were intermediate between these two scales, drawing on a wider politically-motivated community nationally, but with a specific economic focus.

The petition lists provide two important indicators. First, they give a useful guide to the scale of contention and support or protests against established government positions among the membership of the first Liverpool chamber; and, second, how far this related to the wider community. The involvement of the chamber's members and probable members in these petitions, as well as the Corporation's committee of trade members, is shown in the Appendix Tables A.6 – A.7. The overall pattern is summarised in Table 8. Note that the overall scale of chamber petitioners is slightly underestimated since some birth and death dates are not known, which would remove possible petitioners from some years.

Scale and contrasts of support for petitions

With respect to scale, the size of the petitions was similar and relatively small for such a large place as Liverpool. The exception is the Wilkes petition, which was very large and essentially populist, different in kind from the others. There are significant differences between the different categories signing, however. The chamber members as a whole were a large proportion of total petitioners in almost all cases, except for Wilkes (which was hugely populist), and peace and coercion (where they were divided). Hence, the chamber members were a large proportion of the politically active in the city on these petition issues: only lower than 18% of the total petitioners for Wilkes and America, and rising to 30–50% on some issues.

But the known chamber members were generally more active than the probable members. This is, perhaps, not surprising since the known members are chiefly derived from the committee listings (and hence are mostly the most active members). The contrast is particularly marked once the exceptionally large petition on Wilkes and the very divisive petitions on peace and coercion are removed (but recall that the 'probables' sample is drawn from the loyalist petition list of

---

[300] Thomas, 1991.

Table 8 Numbers and proportions of known and probable chamber members, and committee of trade members, signing petitions 1762–80, as a proportion of total signatories (excluding those under 20 at the date, unless actually signing)

Petition	Chamber known Members signing	Chamber probable members signing	Total: all petition signatories	Chamber known plus prob as % of all signing	% of known chamber signing	% of probable chamber signing	% of committee of trade signing
Paper money 1762	8	2	32	31.3	16.3	11.1	33.3
Stamp Act 1765	23	5	115	24.3	45.1	27.7	40.0
Thanks on Stamp Act 1766	25	5	164	18.3	47.2	27.7	27.3
Legal Quays 1766	25	6	88	35.2	46.3	30.0	45.5
Wilkes 1769	22	2	1113	2.2	40.0	10.0	8.3
Free Ports 1773	27	3	55	52.7	45.0	13.0	50.0
Peace 1775	21	0	215	9.8	33.9	0	8.3
Coercion 1775	19	23	470	8.9	30.2	100	75.5
Offices 1780	22	10	177	18.1	34.4	43.5	66.7
Average of all	21.3	6.2	269.9 (164.5 excl. Wilkes)	22.3	38.1	30.4	39.4
Average excluding Wilkes, peace and coercion 1775	21.5	3.5	83.6	28.6	39.9	26.0	43.8

Heywood, which accounts for the 100% figure in 1775). In this case (the bottom row of the table), the known chamber members are more than one and a half times as likely to be active as the probable members.

However, in comparison with the members of the committee of trade, the chamber members were generally slightly less likely to sign several of the petitions. Of those aged over 20 at the time, a very high proportion of the committee of trade signed all petitions, except Wilkes and the peace petition (which were each signed by only one committee member). Thus the committee of trade was also a very politically active group, but its voting was heavily influenced by loyalism in relation to the two most pointed attacks on the government, over Wilkes and peace with America. Loyalism reflected their membership of the Corporation and the dependence between it and the government: it was unwise to expose through a public signature your political opposition to the government if you wanted to retain support from it. This influenced the committee of trade and the probable chamber members much more than the known chamber members, especially the committee, who were much more prepared to make a stand.

Evolution of petitioning

Petitioning activity also reveals a marked evolution in the way in which political views developed among chamber members. Before the American petitions there was a similarity in the level of political activity between the three groups of known, probable chamber members, and the committee of trade; although the chamber, known members and the committee of trade members were usually more engaged than the probable chamber members. For this period, there was thus a degree of alignment of interests, with similar levels of active political commitment between the groups.

The early exception was on Wilkes in 1769, where the petition was handed out in separate sheets placed in different locations, with the sheets then stuck together. One sheet has the names of the main chamber leaders prominently across the top of the central four of the six columns, indicating that they probably signed over these columns before the general display of the petition in order to indicate their own and the chamber's position. These were Richard Kent, Thomas Smythe, Thomas Staniforth, and John Dobson (who signed very prominently in the centre). At the margins, heading columns one and six, were Thomas Crowder and Edward Roberts, who are not known as chamber members. On this sheet, 11 of the chamber members signed, just over half of all the 21 chamber signatories. This pattern is different from all the other petitions, where the chamber members, though often grouped in twos or threes, were spread throughout the lists. On Wilkes the chamber members were thus seeking to give a very public lead.

On America there were again strong local divisions – between peace or military coercion.[301] The government's attitude to the American rebellion was divisive across the country. It would appear that the chamber leaders attempted to place the chamber in a lead position in seeking

---

[301] It should be noted, however, that the probable member sample is not a sample of all probable members, but only those signing the coercion petition; hence, their 100% loyalism is a product of this particular origin of the information. But it seems aligned with their generally weak support for free ports as well as Wilkes, and peace.

peace and concessions from a government that was now committed to war. It is recorded that John Dobson, the Liverpool chamber chair, and Thomas Butterworth Bayley, the Manchester chamber chair, were leading organisers of the peace petition, speaking very fully at a meeting in Lancaster on 9 November 1775.[302] The chamber members were thus seeking to lead in favour of peace, and 21 signed. But this was insufficient to align all members, demonstrating how divisive the American issue had become: 19 chamber members signed the competing petition for use of force. Nevertheless, while the chamber was divided, on this occasion there was sufficient support to allow the chamber's involvement in the conciliation petition to be openly promoted in the *Abstract* in 1777. The petition on offices in 1780 was politically divisive in a different way.

The shifts of opinion are indicated in a simplistic way by noting that the counter-petition from the Corporation on Wilkes in 1769 received about 450 names, compared to the 1,115 supporting Wilkes. In 1775 the degree of opposition was reversed, with the peace petition eliciting only 215 signatures compared with 470 for coercion. By the 1780 petition on offices only 177 signed. Protest was a declining popular cause over the period, partly because the government had increased the stakes: the country was at war and opposition could be interpreted as treason.[303]

An interesting light is shone on the tensions of 1775, by a resolution of a meeting of the Unanimous Society that "ordered that Alexander Nottingham do give unto the mayor of Liverpool, ten guineas for the relief of widows and orphans of the soldiers who died in the service of their country in the present disquiet" [at Lexington and Massachusetts].[304] This resolution, which was for a payment by the Society rather than Nottingham personally. It was signed by 11 people, including Nottingham, as president. This included chamber members Rawlinson, Brooks junior and John Chorley (who was the Society's secretary). Three others were members of the committee of trade, and all the remaining four were Common Councillors. It is notable that eight of these signed the coercion petition, but not three of the four chamber members (Chorley and Rawlinson were peace petitioners, and Nottingham signed neither petition; only Brooks junior signed for coercion). The resolution was an attempt by loyalists to use the Unanimous Society to influence its members and others to support the government. Nottingham clearly sought to remain neutral but his hand was forced.

---

[302] Cumberland Pacquet, 16 November 1775; see also Bradley, 1990, p 343.
[303] Thomas, 1991.
[304] LRO 367 UNA/1, 4 November 1775.

This tension may explain why the Society saw no new chamber members after 1774, and ceased to exist after 1778.

Religious dimensions to political activism?

It has already been noted that dissenters were often politically more active than Anglicans at this time and, in Liverpool, this has been found to be particularly true among the merchants, especially after 1775.[305] Table 9 shows that this is also true of the known chamber members, where dissenters were much more active than the Anglicans in petitioning on all, except for the coercion and offices petitions of 1775 and 1780: between one and half and two times more likely to petition than the Anglicans (average 1.5 times). This difference is statistically significant.[306] On average, the majority of dissenters were likely to petition, while only about one-third of Anglicans would do so. Signatories for the Stamp Act and legal quays included about three-quarters of all dissenters in the chamber, and two-thirds for the peace petition. In contrast, the level of petitioning activity by the Anglican known chamber members was remarkably similar throughout the period, being lower only for paper money and peace. For the probable chamber members, by contrast, the dissenter members were less likely to petition (but this group is drawn from a loyalist sample), while the overall rate of petitioning is much lower than for known members, as noted earlier.

Thus, while it is correct to conclude that the chamber was cross-sectarian and provides no evidence of a dominant religious ideology, its dissenter members played a disproportionately prominent role in political activism. It would appear that they were a strong force in propelling the overall activism of the chamber to pursue its reform agenda.

Petitioners, the chamber and the business community

The petitions also indicate how the politically active and the chamber's membership interrelated. Only the known members are analysed here. Comparison of the type of business activity of the petitioners is shown in Table 10, using directory sources, for a sample of three of the petitions.[307] The breakdown of petitioners by business sectors is quite similar to that of the chamber's known members (particularly the

---

[305] Bradley, 1990, eg pp 284–9 and Table 10.4, p 400.
[306] Small numbers and cell frequencies make statistical testing difficult; but a binomial sign test rejects the null hypothesis of no difference between religions in activism at the 90% level (probability 0.090), while a Fisher test gives a value of 34.9 with 8 d.f., rejecting the null hypothesis at the 99% level.
[307] There are a few cases where the signature is indistinct and thus cannot be used.

Table 9 Level of petitioning activity compared between Anglican and dissenting chamber members. For each cell the table shows the number of chamber members signing a petition out of the number of chambers members of that religion alive and aged over 20 at the time, with the percentage signing in brackets

Petition	Known chamber members		Probable chamber members	
	Anglicans	**Dissenters**	**Anglicans**	**Dissenters**
1 Paper money 1762	5/34 (14.7)	3/11 (27.3)	2/14(14.3)	0/4 (-)
2 Stamp Act 1765	13/34 (38.2)	10/13 (76.9)	5/14 (35.7)	0/4 (-)
3 Stamp Act thanks 1766	15/35 (42.9)	9/14 (64.3)	4/14 (28.6)	1/4 (25.0)
4 Legal Quays 1766	15/35 (42.9)	11/15 (73.3)	6/16 (37.5)	0/4 (-)
5 Wilkes 1769	15/36 (41.7)	7/15 (46.7)	1/16 (6.3)	1/4 (25.0)
6 Free ports 1773	17/39 (43.6)	10/17 (58.8)	2/17 (11.7)	0/4 (-)
7 Peace 1775	9/40 (22.5)	12/18 (66.7)	0/18 (-)	0/5 (-)
8 Coercion 1775	14/41 (34.1)	5/18 (27.8)	18/18 (100)	5/5 (100.0)
9 Offices 1780	15/42 (35.7)	6/18 (33.3)	10/18 (55.6)	1/5 (20.0)
Average (%)	**35.1**	**52.5**	**33.1**	**20.5**
Average (excluding peace and coercion) (%)	**37.3**	**54.4**	**27.5**	**10.3**

proportion of merchants and bankers), but the general petitioners have many more manufacturers/artisans, and a much stronger presence of retailers, victuallers, lawyers and other sectors who are not known members of the chamber. The merchants and bankers, therefore, seem to have been leading political forces as both petitioners and in the chamber. But the chamber did not present the smaller artisans and had a low proportion of manufacturers.

A similar comparison is possible of the business structure, which shows about 20% of the petitioners to be partnership businesses. This proportion is much lower than the chamber's known or probable members (with, respectively, 89% and 82% partnerships). Nevertheless, the petitioners represent a large proportion of the total number of partnership businesses in the city at the time. The directories suggest that there were about 105–150 partnerships in 1766, 1775 and 1780. The petitioners included about 41 partnerships in each year. This is about 25–40% of the total, of which the chamber members who signed

Table 10 Business sector of all petitioners and known chamber members for petitions in 1766, 1775 and 1780

	1766 Stamp Act thanks			1775 Peace			1780 Offices		
	No	%	Of which chamber No	No	%	Of which chamber No	No	%	Of which chamber No
Merchant	101	63.9	20	68	34.7	13	74	47.7	15
Manufacturer/ artisan	27	17.1	2	42	21.4	2	23	14.8	2
Victualler	-	-	-	9	4.6	-	4	2.6	-
Retail/grocer	13	8.2	-	18	9.2	-	9	5.8	-
Captain	6	3.8	-	13	6.6	-	2	1.3	-
Bank/broker	3	1.9	3	5	2.6	4	11	7.1	5
Warehouse	3	1.9	-	6	3.1	-	4	2.6	-
Attorney	4	2.5	-	5	2.6	-	11	7.1	-
Gent/Esq	-	-	-	14	7.0	-	11	7.1	-
Other	1	0.6	-	16	8.2	-	6	3.9	-
Identifiable signatures	158	(96.3)	25	196	(91.2)	19	155	(88.1)	22
Total signatures	164	-		215		-	176	-	-

the petition were over half in each case. Thus the petitioners disproportionately represented the larger diversified businesses, but the chamber members were an even larger proportion of these leading partnership businesses. The largest businesses were thus more likely to be politically active as petitioners, within which chamber members were even more active.

These conclusions must be treated with caution for all sorts of reasons of uncertainty in the information sources and the sizes of samples. But they clearly show a chamber that had an active political membership on a wide range of 'reform' issues. For the American question, however, the known membership was divided. The probable membership, as noted earlier, was generally less socially engaged and networked than the known membership, was strongly loyalist, and was hence perhaps more willing to be influenced or subject to local pressures on issues like Wilkes and coercion where loyalism to the government was exposed – remembering that all petitions were public documents open to view by all locally, and when received by the government.

13
Demise

The chamber appears to have become markedly less active after Samuel Green's death in November 1792. It may de facto have become inactive at that time. However, as discussed above, some sort of halting activity by leading members probably continued under John Tarleton until the chamber fell into final abeyance by the end of 1796, after which no further records have been found. The reasons for this final demise are uncertain, but fall into six categories: general pressures; turnover of the membership; the variable commitments of John Tarleton; the changing attitude of the Corporation; the availability of alternatives; and, particularly, the foundation of the Liverpool American chamber of commerce in 1801.

General pressures

In other chambers, the period from the late 1790s up to 1815 was a quiet one, and some other chambers certainly fell into abeyance for a time, eg Manchester and Birmingham. Even New York failed to meet between 1806 and 1817.[308] The Jay Treaty of 1794–5 led to rapprochement with, and gradual resolution of, the commercial disputes with America, which removed one of the chamber's initial main concerns.

---

[308] Bishop, 1918, p 51.

In addition, it is quite understandable that many merchants and traders were preoccupied with survival of their businesses as wars in Europe came to dominate national life, and many merchants in Liverpool struggled to survive.[309] Several of the leading Liverpool chamber members enlisted and went to the continent.[310] As a result of the wars, much trade was forced into convoys, with embargoes on other shipping movements. This trade became controlled by the Admiralty's organisation, which undermined the need for a chamber, as each merchant dealt separately with Admiralty administrators.[311]

Membership turnover

There was natural turnover and erosion of the chamber membership with time. As in any voluntary organisation, its continued vitality relied on recruiting new and committed members to succeed those who moved, resigned or died. In Liverpool we have noted how the early years were dominated by 20–30 key members. When these were no longer available or committed, there would be a need for new blood. By the time of Samuel Green's death, in 1792, at least seven of the original known members were dead. By 1796 at least 13 of the other main committee members had died, including five of the 20–30 most important of the committee noted in Table 2 (of which Dobson, Nottingham and the Heywoods would have been critical losses).[312] In addition, Clayton Tarleton, who had become a supporter within the Corporation, died in 1797.

Others moved or retired. Matthew Nicholson moved from Liverpool to Manchester in 1785 to run the Heywoods Bank there (joining the Manchester chamber instead).[313] Francis Ingram moved to establish a banking business in Wakefield in 1790.[314] Thomas Smyth, a partner with Charles Caldwell, left Liverpool with Caldwell when their bank failed in 1793.[315] The deaths and movements of many others are not known, but more would have lost commitment over the later years of the chamber's life.

---

[309] Hughes, 1906; Mariner, 1951.
[310] Eg in 1794 Nicholas Ashton; Bamber Gasgoyne MP also enlisted: LRO 920 TAR 4/68; 27 October 1794.
[311] See Rodger, 2004; Redford, 1934, chapter 3.
[312] Full genealogical cover of the chamber members is beyond the scope of this book, but the deaths of those that can be traced are shown in Appendix Tables A.3 and A.4.
[313] Nicholson, 1928, pp 64–5, 132–5; Bennett, 2011, chapter 4.
[314] Hughes, 1906, p 133–5.
[315] Hughes, 1906, p 87.

Developments in the Corporation

A major stimulus to the chamber's formation had been anger with the Corporation. But when the Corporation's committee of trade became more co-operative with the chamber after 1783–4, and when the Corporation itself appears to have worked more effectively to include the chamber interests under Clayton Tarleton from 1793, some of the need for a chamber was diminished. The Corporation de facto took over some of its activities. This was reinforced by the 1793 banking crisis which forced Liverpool interests to work together, at least for a time. Once the chamber's main facilitator, Samuel Green, died in late 1792, a more supportive Corporation may have eroded the commitment of some chamber members to sustain their own body. This would be especially true with the death of their most vigorous members, Dobson in 1791, and Arthur and Benjamin Heywood in 1795, who were the members with the strongest visceral dislike for the Common Council, sufficient to stimulate their anger and energies during the foundation process.

John Tarleton's divisive position

We also have the situation that John Tarleton, as we have seen, took on multiple roles that brought conflicts of interest. He sought to take on a central role after Green's death, having been elected as an MP for Seaford in the same year, 1792. But he was clearly torn between his loyalties to the government in order to further his political career, and his support for local business views. He did not fairly represent the merchants' interests on the East India or merchant seamen's issues; he was opposed to open trade with Ireland when it appears that the chamber and wider business community outside the Corporation was in favour. He initially opposed the Bill for Corporation loan notes in 1793. He was a supporter of coercion on America in 1775, which was divisive between chamber members. He was also compromised by his identification as a prominent opponent of slave trade abolition, an issue on which the chamber had sought to stand back. These conflicted positions would be apparent to the chamber members, so that his attempted role as a major facilitator of the chamber's voice would have been problematic.

The Tarletons had never been popular with some chamber members. There was evidently a support faction for them in the chamber, since Thomas had been a committee member for five of the first nine years, and John became a committee member in 1785–6, but John was a relatively unconnected figure through the networks shown in Figures 2 and

3. Similarly, when their father, John senior, was exploring support for standing as MP for Liverpool in 1767–8, only one probable chamber member (Samuel Appleton) was involved in the initial approach to invite him, on 18 July 1767. This grew to two probable and four known members as supporters by 23 July.[316] However, those willing to subscribe never extended beyond Thomas Case and William Earle, with Earle the only one willing to be on his committee.[317] The committee of trade members were stronger supporters, including four to five throughout the 1767 discussions. Tarleton senior received the most involvement from the future chamber members at a meeting on 6 May 1768. Then seven known and four probable chamber members, and five committee of trade members, are listed as attending the meeting (which now included the Heywoods). But, of these, only Thomas Case was willing to give financial support (though this support was questionable since he was away at Chester at the time), all the other chamber members explicitly declined to do so. Indeed, of 50 attending the meeting, only 12 promised financial support (almost entirely Common Council members, including John Sparling), but even this was conditional "provided it was generally adopted".[318] When he and his supporters tried to get to the hustings to initiate his candidacy there was intimidation by potters waving blubber-knives which prevented him.[319] Some chamber members were probably linked to this, especially the Rathbones, but also Chaffers, Dobson and the Lakes who all favoured the rival candidate (William Meredith), and had links to the potters who were primarily involved. Thus, even at an early date, the Tarletons were not consensus figures, with some chamber members definitely strongly opposed, especially to both John senior and junior.

The dénouement would have come in 1796 when chamber member John Tarleton junior contested the Liverpool general election against his brother Banastre, which the latter won. Banastre was the incumbent, a popular war hero of the American campaigns, who was relatively independent, supported by the Heywoods, generally helped Liverpool interests, but followed leading opposition figure Charles Fox, and usually voted with the opposition. The government Tories encouraged John Tarleton to stand against him, although John was already MP for Seaford.[320] This was John's chance to enter Liverpool politics as his father had attempted in 1767–8. He might have felt this would be easy since Banastre's "ignorance of mercantile matters and love of pleasure

[316] Nottingham, Brooks jun, W. Earle and T Case; LRO 920 TAR/3/1; TAR/3/2.
[317] LRO 920 TAR/3/6 and 11.
[318] LRO 920 TAR/3/11.
[319] Liverpool Chronicle, 24 March 1768; Troughton, 1810, p 145; Brooke, 1853, p 303; Boney, 1957.
[320] DNB, 1898, 2004; Rathbone, 1913, p.68; Thorne, *History of Parliament*.

made him no very efficient representative of an important commercial town like Liverpool",[321] although both he and John had been stalwart opponents of slave trade abolition.[322] Certainly John played up his commercial credentials and the efforts he had put into representing Liverpool interests since he had become an MP in 1792. Indeed, it appears that John's activities as advocate/facilitator of the Liverpool merchants' and chamber members' interests, as well as in other fields, from 1792 onwards were all geared towards fighting an election in Liverpool. Thorne interprets his actions as a "go-between of Pitt and the Liverpool merchants",[323] working with the mayor. He describes himself in a 1796 pamphlet as, "a decided supporter of the general measures of the present administration. ... Of my attention to the interests of my fellow townsmen ... they will be ascertained by a reference to those who have given me the opportunity of exerting my service".[324] This reads very much as referring to the chamber and other merchant interests whom he calls on to vote for him, though he does not mention the chamber explicitly. In comparison, John described Banastre as worthy, with military expertise, but John would be "like a blushing rose upon a barren forest".[325]

Whatever John Tarleton's merits, this contest against his brother seems to have deepened a family rift that had been developing for some time. In about 1791 Clayton Tarleton had left the family firm of Tarleton and Backhouse, run with his brothers John and Thomas, and probable chamber member Daniel Backhouse, to start out on his own with William Rigg.[326] While John and Clayton continued to work together during Clayton's mayoralty, there must have been tensions due to the pro-government line followed by John, perhaps most evident and public when John opposed the 1793 Corporation Act to issue notes during the banking crisis. But John's 1796 contest against his third brother Banastre was an extreme family test, that was judged 'unbrotherly'. One of the squibs in the election states: "In your conduct towards your brother, I accuse you of having transgressed all those rules and obligations which link together relation and relation, man and man ... unrestrained by any filial consideration for your mother, whose peace of mind has already received a severe sock from your brutal and unnatural conduct."[327] This reads as his brother Clayton's views. However, John, in a following squib "resolved not to shrink back". The conflict

[321] DNB, 1898, 2004.
[322] Drescher, 1986, p 81–2; Sanderson, 1989.
[323] Thorne, *History of Parliament*, p 336.
[324] Poll book and squibs, p 4: LRO H324.242.PAR.
[325] op. cit., squib by 'A Dick Sam'.
[326] Pope, 1970, vol. 2, p 351.
[327] This is signed by 'An Observer', 27 May 1796; op. cit. p 45.

was deep. He received no bequest from either Clayton or his mother when both died in the following year, 1797.[328]

In the 1796 election, the turnout was low, not many of the known chamber members voted (only eight) and, of these, only John Bolton voted for John Tarleton,[329] which suggests that he had lost almost all support from the chamber members. Indeed, Arthur Heywood remained a prominent supporter of Banastre and chaired his celebration dinner in 1791.[330] Hence, there were a number of reasons why John became discredited, conflicted and compromised which would have lost him the support of the chamber. But he seems to have been one of the main forces acting as a collective advocate after Green's death, so this produced a dilemma. Once he lost the election, John appears to have lost interest in the city and the chamber; they were no longer useful for his purposes, and he withdrew from general public life.[331] This must have hastened the chamber's demise.

Available alternatives

There were also other important developments in Liverpool at this time that provided alternatives. One important development was the opening of the Tontine Hotel (Bates) by Ryan and his chamber companions in 1784. Based on a separate subscription membership, this would have undermined the need for a separate chamber after 1784. Similarly, the issuing of the prospectus for the Athenaeum in 1797, which offered a meeting room for merchants (and others) that had been sought by the chamber in 1777, provided a further alternative venue. Indeed, the initial impetus for many of the founders of the Athenaeum was to provide a better facility than the Bates Hotel Newsroom.[332] Its initial subscription of ten guineas per head and two guineas per annum was similar to the chamber's. By January 1799 the Athenaeum's building was opened, with a newsroom and meeting room. Twenty of the known chamber members, and three of the probable members, were early subscribers to the Athenaeum, over 40% of the chamber's known total surviving membership.[333]

Other representative bodies also developed, which Redford has suggested offered the main business associations in the town. There had been the Africa Committee since 1750; and a Liverpool West India

---

[328] John Tarleton, DNB, 2004, p 786; Cheshire Sheaf, August 1930.
[329] Liverpool election pollbook, 1796.
[330] Williamsons Advertiser 27 June 1791.
[331] DNB, 2004.
[332] Brooke, 1853, p 429.
[333] Athenaeum membership listed in Carrick and Ashton, 1997, Appendix 2; see also Appendix Table A.3 and A.4.

Association was founded in 1799.[334] Also national trade bodies became more numerous at this time; important among them for Liverpool was the Society of Shipowners of Great Britain, established in 1802.[335] The Liverpool Marine Society was founded as an independent body in 1789, a counterpart of the Jersey chamber's activities, to support seamen and their families, removing a possible role for the chamber (and chamber members were involved with it, and Thomas Staniforth was its first president).[336]

A successor chamber?

Perhaps most important, however, in 1801 the American chamber of commerce in Liverpool was founded, with the rules drafted by William Rathbone, one of Joseph Rathbone's relatives.[337] This successfully came to undertake many of the most significant lobby activities that the earlier chamber had formerly done. From 1815 this was on a much greater scale, when it opened a lobbying office in London.[338] It is notable that five of the earlier chamber's known committee members and four of the probable members were, in 1801, founding members of the American chamber,[339] while other founders were strongly connected with the businesses of the former chamber's members. Given the lapse of time and probable death or withdrawal from business of many of the earlier chamber's members, this shows a considerable overlap, which suggests significant continuity between the two chamber bodies.

It is also notable that the American chamber started with a subscription model similar to that which the chamber had evolved towards, charging a two guinea annual subscription. But it switched from this to a levy based on the trade duty in 1811; this ranged from one farthing to 10s per item,[340] and is a reminder of the early proposal in the first chamber's *Deed* to use trade duties as its subscription base.

It is also possible that the American chamber was founded specifically because of the 'capture' of the earlier chamber by the Tarleton interest in the 1790s, and/or its increasingly close alignment with the Corporation and the government. The Rathbones, who were key founders of the American chamber, were bitter opponents of the

[334] Redford, 1934; LRO 380WES/1/1.
[335] Society of Shipowners of Great Britain, 1807, *Collection of Reports and Papers on Navigation or Trade,* J Stockdale, London.
[336] Brooke, 1853, p 393.
[337] See Checkland, 1958, p 145 n.20.
[338] Henderson, 1933a, 1993b; Checkland, 1958.
[339] They were Carruthers, Corrie, Earle, Hodgson, and Myers; and probable members Backhouse, Blundell, Parke, and the son of Robert Grimshaw; LRO 380 AME/4; Minute Book of the American Chamber of Commerce: LRO B80 AME/4. Its treasurer up to 1838 was John Cropper, a close associate of Leyland: Liverpool Maritime Museum archives D/CR/2/7.
[340] Henderson, 1933a.

Tarletons, with William Rathbone one of the leading radicals in the city, viscerally opposed to the Corporation.[341]

Certainly the same concerns occupied the American chamber and the earlier chamber, especially the docks. The Corporation had been compelled in 1762 to put the docks under trustees, but this objective was subverted by drawing trustees only from the Common Council. The chamber's agitation over 1774–96 evidences grievances over this structure. With the expansion of the docks, the concerns were bound to become progressively greater. The continued expansion of the docks provided the Corporation with a strengthening monopoly over landing and fees; it also restricted shipbuilding sites and eventually forced this activity to the Wirral shore. The American chamber was at the front of a Bill in 1825 to remove the Council's hold over the trustees altogether, and achieved a structure where eight of 21 trustees were externally elected from the port users at large. In 1851 the American chamber renewed its efforts through promoting a Reform Bill for the docks to reduce the Council's trustees to 25%, and achieved a further reduction to 12 of 24. But only in 1858 was the objective achieved of constituting a more general body, the Mersey Docks and Harbour Board, where the majority were port users. This was the result of vigorous pressure from the American chamber, the new Liverpool chamber founded in 1850, the Manchester chamber, and the port users.[342]

Final abeyance and lost memory

We thus have evidence of friction among leading chamber members (between the Tarletons, and of the Tarletons with others), the conflicts of interest of John Tarleton, his discredit (because of his 1793 credit crisis behaviour and 1796 election antics), the death of the secretary in 1792, the increasingly close alignment of the Corporation with the merchants during and after the 1793 crisis, the death or turnover of many other members, pressures of the wars, and the development of effective alternatives, especially the American chamber. Despite these indications, we as yet have no firm evidence of when Liverpool's first chamber finally fell into abeyance. It was probably about 1796, when Tarleton withdrew from the scene, or 1797, when the Athenaeum got under way. Certainly it was long enough before the modern chamber's re-foundation in 1849–50 for all memory to have been erased, as no mention of the first chamber occurs in any of the later Liverpool chamber's records.

[341] Rathbone, 1913 p 101 ff.; Aspinall, 1852.
[342] Liverpool chamber minutes, 1857–8; Picton, 1903, vol.1, pp 551–607; Mountfield, 1965; Power, 1997; Milne, 2000; see also Hyde, 1971, pp 76–7 and ff.

14
Conclusion

This book has given an account of the first Liverpool chamber of commerce, and also sought to set its establishment within the context of national and local developments of the time. It has sought to construct the story of Liverpool's chamber through a multi-layered account, assessing purpose, structure, critical conjunctions of forces leading to foundation, and the personalities and networks that underpinned it.

This has led to an unravelling of what academics might call the repertoires of contention within the city at this time. A more extensive analysis of these networks and repertoires across the whole Atlantic world is provided in the author's study of all the chambers of commerce, to be published in 2011. This shows Liverpool as a pivotal case within the global economic regime of the day. Most significant, the chamber's launch against the strong opposition from the city's Corporation can be seen as part of the emerging challenges to the aristocracy and self-elected corporations of the pre-Reform state. The leading members of the chamber comprised a group of mercantile individuals who sought to exert a new and different 'voice' on behalf of the local business community. It is not surprising, therefore, that the Corporation sought to squash it. The chamber's history, therefore, throws important insights into the development of national political attitudes and local interests of the time.

Liverpool chamber's significance in business history

The creation of the first Liverpool chamber of commerce was an important initiative in the history of British business organisations: it was the third or fourth chamber in the British Isles and the first in a major port. Its creation demonstrates the important role of the Atlantic trade and emerging international tensions with America. The chamber's history illustrates the emergence of one of the first new 'deliberated', organised and sustained provincial 'voices', seeking to be heard directly in Westminster, and offering a counterpoint to the interests of the great London merchants and the Corporations. This independent voice was, however, tempered with recognition that Liverpool was still a long way behind London as a port, and needed to work with the merchants and interests there, and in other cities (especially Bristol and Glasgow) trading in north America, Africa and the West Indies.

The collaboration with these other merchants in the great lobbies of 1766 on the Stamp Act, and in 1775 for compromise and peace in America, shows Liverpool as a key player in an emerging national voice for business at Westminster. The development of this Liverpool voice in national politics is covered more fully elsewhere.[343] However, from the discussion here it is evident that Liverpool was acting as a strong and independent force on American and Atlantic trade lobbies. Especially over 1785–7 this was, like Glasgow and Dublin, distinct in acting with, but also independently of, the General Chamber and its provincial delegates and committees when Pitt's Irish propositions and the Treaty with France were being negotiated. Manchester, Birmingham and the other chambers and committees involved directly with the General Chamber worked more closely with the opposition and had to regroup when the General Chamber failed. Liverpool's evolution, therefore, illustrates an important chapter in chamber development: one of the bodies bound up so closely in the Atlantic economy that it tended to stay outside the manufacturing focus of the General Chamber. This was despite its relations with the Manchester chamber and industrial Lancashire, though it shared similar concerns covering naval convoys. The similarity of Liverpool with the Glasgow chamber is striking and to be expected from their similar trading histories. There are also similarities with Bristol, but in this case the local body was the Merchant Venturers, a body which was part of the 'old', as well as attempting to be a new way of representing business interests. Liverpool, Glasgow and Bristol were in close contact with each other on several policy issues

[343] Bennett, 2011, Chapters 4 and 9.

and helped each other's parliamentary lobbies, working separately and distinctly from the General Chamber.

The chamber's significance for municipal and local history

Liverpool's first chamber of commerce is also of significance because of the light it throws on conflicts with the Corporation. The Corporation sought to embody the chamber concept within the Corporation itself in early 1774 but, after the chamber was established in June, it set up a rival committee of trade in 1775. This survived until 1794, coming to an end at about the same time as the chamber. But the activities of the two bodies, after initial rivalry, seem to have been largely accommodated. Indeed, analysis of the political alignment of the members of the committee and the chamber show the two to be very similar on most economic concerns, and only differed where explicit political challenge to the government arose (as with Wilkes and concessions to America), over the issues of the slave trade, and over open trade with the West Indies and Ireland.

The establishment of the chamber thus appears to represent a period of significant change among the main mercantile power brokers of the period. Undoubtedly, further research on these personalities would illuminate the commercial structures further. But it seems clear that the chamber represented a broad group of major merchants and trade activities, with an emphasis on large firms with an international dimension. Many of these businesses were very diversified and developing broader bases; almost all the key banking interests were represented in positions of influence in the chamber. The future, especially when the slavery abolition movement got under way, was in diversification. The chamber, therefore, illustrates important indications of an early shift of local business leadership reflecting new trades and more advanced capitalist structures of banking and industrial co-operation through partnerships (which may be seen as the early precursors of the future limited companies and trading groups).

Assimilation and demise

However, individual interests evolve and it appears that a 'new guard' had supplanted some of the old guard on the Corporation by the mid-1780s. The Corporation itself sought to align with the chamber's concerns, at least for a short period. This parallels the evolution of other significant Liverpool bodies such as the parish Vestry. By the 1790s, when the brothers Clayton Tarleton (as mayor) and John Tarleton (as probable chamber chair) were working closely together, the Corporation's committee of trade was allowed to fall into abeyance, the Common Council and chamber were voicing similar concerns, and the need for an independent chamber diminished. Other alternatives also developed, including the Bates Tontine Hotel meeting rooms, the Athenaeum, and especially the Liverpool American chamber. The tensions between the business community and the Corporation remained, however, as evident in the subsequent campaigns over management of the docks by the American chamber and the Liverpool chamber of 1850. The first chamber thus appears to have fallen into abeyance by 1796–7, and perhaps de facto soon after Green's death in 1792. When the new chamber was founded in 1849–50, no memory of the former body existed. It is hoped that this book now fills that gap in lost history.

Your comments:

Nothing is simple in Liverpool's economic and political history, and it would be foolish to claim that this book has been able to answer all the questions that can be asked, or that every detail has been uncovered. Some aspects, such as the genealogy of members and their attitudes, require considerable further research. Other areas may remain uncertain. But this book provides the context to develop further insights and for the discovery and interpretation of other documents. The modern chamber is to maintain a web-based resource to allow comments and further information to be added on this early history. Constructive comments are welcomed on info@liverpoolchamber.org.uk.

Acknowledgements

This book was developed as part of a national historical study of chambers of commerce, which has been supported by British Academy small grants. I am particularly grateful for the help of the Library Company of Philadelphia, to Joan Hanford, librarian of the Liverpool Athenaeum, to the staff of the Liverpool Record Office, and for generous help with archives from the other sources cited.

Figure 1 was drawn by Philip Stickler and Figures 2 and 3 by David Watson, both of Cambridge University Cartographic Unit.

References

Aspinall, J. (an old stager) (1852) *Liverpool a few years since,* Deighton and Haughton Liverpool.

Baines, T. (1852) *History of the commerce and town of Liverpool,* Longman Brown, London.

Bargar, B. D. (1956) Matthew Boulton and the Birmingham Petition of 1775, *William and Mary Quarterly,* 13 (3), 26–39.

Barker, T. C. (1949) The Sankey Navigation: The first Lancashire canal, *Transactions of the Historic Society of Lancashire and Cheshire,* 100, 121–154.

Barker, T.C. and Harris, J.R. (1959) *A Merseyside town in the industrial revolution: St. Helens 1750–1900,* Frank Case, London.

Behrendt, S.D. (1990) The Captains of the British Slave Trade from 1785–1807, *Transactions Historic Society of Lancashire and Cheshire,* 140, 79–140.

Belchem, J. (ed.) (1992) *Popular politics, riot and labour: Essays in Liverpool history,* University of Liverpool Press.

Bennett, R. J. (2011) *Local business voice: the history of chambers of commerce in Britain, Ireland and Revolutionary America 1760–2011,* Oxford University Press.

Bishop, J. B. (1918) *A chronicle of one hundred and fifty years: the chamber of commerce of the State of New York,* Charles Scribner, New York.

Boardman, J. (1871) *Liverpool table-talk a hundred years ago; or a history of Gore's Directory,* second edition of 1766 original, Henry Young, Liverpool

Boney, K. (1957) *Liverpool porcelain of the Eighteenth Century and its makers,* Portman Press, London.

Bradley, J. E. (1986) *Popular politics and the American Revolution in England: petitions, the Crown, and public opinion,* Mercer University Press, Macon, Georgia.

Bradley, J. E. (1990) *Religion, revolution, and English radicalism: Nonconformity in Eighteenth Century politics and society,* Cambridge University Press.

Brewer, J. (1989) *The sinews of power: War, money and the English state, 1688–1783,* Unwin Hyman, London.

Brooke, R. (1853) Liverpool as it was during the last quarter of the eighteenth century 1775–1780, J. Mawdsley, Liverpool.

Carrick, N. and Ashton, E. L. (1997) *The Athenaeum Liverpool, 1797–1997,* The Athenaeum, Liverpool.

Chandler, G. (1964) *Four centuries of banking*, Batsford, London.

Checkland, S. G. (1952) Economic attitudes in Liverpool 1793–1807, *Economic History Review*, 5, 58–75.

Checkland, S. G. (1958) American versus West Indian traders in Liverpool 1793–1815, *Journal of Economic History*, 18, 141–60.

Checkland, S. G. (1971) *The Gladstones: A family biography, 1764–1851*, Cambridge University Press.

Civin, J. (2003) Slaves, sati and sugar: Constructing imperial identity through Liverpool petition struggles, Chapter 10, pp 187–205, in J. Hoppit (ed.) *Parliaments, nations and identities in Britain and Ireland, 1660–1850*, Manchester University Press.

Craig, R. and Jarvis, R. (1967) *Liverpool registry of merchant ships*, Chetham Society, Manchester.

Cullen, L. M. (1983) Princes and Pirates: The Dublin Chamber of Commerce 1783–1983, Dublin Chamber of Commerce, 126 pp.

Donnan, E. (1931) *Documents illustrative of the history of the slave trade to America*, Carnegie Institution, Washington DC.

Drescher, S. (1986) *Capitalism and anti-slavery: British mobilisation in comparative perspective*, Macmillan, London.

Earle, T. A. (1890) Earle of Allerton Tower, Transactions of the Historic Society of Lancashire and Cheshire, XLII, 15–76.

Evans, G. E. (1887) *A history of Renshaw Street Chapel*, C. Green, London.

Fox-Bourne, H. R. (1886) *English Merchants,* Chatto and Windus, London.

Gatty, C. T. (1882) *The Mayer Collection: The Liverpool Potteries*, Liverpool Art Club.

Gay, N. (1799), *Strictures on the proposed union between great Britain and Ireland; with occasional remarks*, London.

Gilson Martin W. A. (1950), *A Century of Liverpool's Commerce: Centenary history of Liverpool Chamber of Commerce* (1850–1950), Charles Birchall and Sons, Liverpool.

Gonner, E. C. K. (1896) Municipal bank notes in Liverpool, 1793–5, *Economic Journal*, 6, 23, 484–487.

Haggerty, S. (2002) The structure of the trading community in Liverpool 1760–1810, *Transactions of the Historic Society of Lancashire and Cheshire*, 151, 97–125.

Haggerty, S. (2006) *The British-Atlantic trading community, 1760–1810: Men, women, and the distribution of goods*, Brill, Boston.

Henderson, W. O. (1933a) The American Chamber of Commerce for the Port of Liverpool, 1801–1908, *Transactions of the Historic Society of Lancashire and Cheshire*, 85, 1–61.

Henderson, W. O. (1933b) The Liverpool Office in London, *Economica*, 18, 473–479.

Hext, J. (ed.) (1965) *The Staniforth diary: A visit to Cornwall in 1800*, D. Bradford Barton, Truro.

Horley, E. (1881) The Mock Corporation of Sephton, 2 parts, *Transactions of the Historic Society of Lancashire and Cheshire*, 33, 223–246; 34, 25–38.

Howman, B. (2007) Abolitionism in Liverpool, Chapter 10, pp 277–296, in D. Richardson, S. Schwarz and A. Tibbles (eds.) *Liverpool and transatlantic slavery*, Liverpool University Press.

Hughes, J. (1906) *Liverpool Banks and Bankers 1760–1837,* Henry Young & Sons, Liverpool.

Hyde, F. E., Bradbury, B. P. and Mariner, S. (1951) The port of Liverpool and the crisis of 1793, *Economica*, 18, 363–378.

Hyde, F. E. (1971) *Liverpool and the Mersey: An economic history of the port 1700–1970*, David and Charles, Newton Abbot.

Ilersic, A. R. and Liddle, P. F. B. (1960) *Parliament of Commerce: The story of the Association of British Chambers of Commerce 1860–1960*, Association of British Chambers of Commerce, London.

Inikori, J. E. (1981) Market structure and the profits of the British African trade in the late Eighteenth Century, *Journal of Economic History*, 41 (4), 745–776.

Jarvis, R.C. (1954) *Customs letter-books of the Port of Liverpool, 1711–1813*, Chetham Society, 3rd series, 6, Manchester.

Jarvis, R.C. (1969) Eighteenth century London shipping, pp 414–7 in A. E. J. Hollaender and W. Kellaway (eds.) *Studies in London History*, Hodder and Stoughton, London.

Kemp, B. (1953) Crewe's Act, 1782, *English Historical Review*, 68, 258–263.

Littler, D. (1996) The Earle collection: records of a Liverpool family of merchants, *Transactions of the Historic Society of Lancashire and Cheshire*, 146, 193–106.

Liverpool Chamber of Commerce (1997) *A Short History of the Liverpool Chamber of Commerce*, Liverpool.

Longmore, J. (2007) 'Cemented by the blood of the negro'? The impact of the slave trade on eighteenth century Liverpool, Chapter 8, pp 227–251, in D. Richardson, S. Schwarz and A. Tibbles (eds.) *Liverpool and transatlantic slavery*, Liverpool University Press.

Mariner, S. (1951) The Port of Liverpool and the crisis of 1793, *Economica*, 18, 368–9.

Mathews, G. W. (1941) John Bolton, a Liverpool merchant, 1765–1837, *Transactions of the Historic Society of Lancashire and Cheshire*, 93, 98–103.

Menzies, E. M. (1972) The freeman voter in Liverpool, 1802–1835, *Transactions of the Historic Society of Lancashire and Cheshire*, 124, 85–107.

Meteyard, E. (1866) *The life of Josiah Wedgwood*, 2 vols., Hurst and Blackett, London.

Milligan, E. H. (2007) *Biographical dictionary of British Quakers in commerce and industry 1775–1920*, Sessions Book Trust, York.

Milne, C. J. (2000) *Trade and traders in mid-Victorian Liverpool: mercantile business and the making of a modern port*, Liverpool University Press.

Morgan, K. (2000) Business networks in the British export trade to North America, 1750–1800, pp 36–62, in J.J. McCusker and K. Morgan (eds.), *The Early Modern Atlantic Economy*, Cambridge University Press.

Morgan, K. (ed.) (2007) *The Bright-Meyer Papers, A Bristol-West India Connection, 1732–1837*, Oxford University Press.

Mountfield, S. (165) *Western Gateway: A history of the Mersey Docks and Harbour Board*, Liverpool University Press.

Muir, R. (1907) *A History of Liverpool*, Liverpool University Press.

Muir, R. and Platt, E. M. (1906) *A History of Municipal Government in Liverpool*, Liverpool University Press.

Nicholson, F. (1928) *Memorials of the Nicholson family*, private printing, Titus Wilson, Kendal.

Nightingale, B. (1893) *Lancashire nonconformity*, six volumes, John Heywood, Liverpool.

Oakley, C. A. (1983) *Our illustrious forbears: The Glasgow Chamber of Commerce 1783–1983*, Blackie and Sons, Glasgow.

Olson, A. G. (1973) *Anglo-American Politics 1660–1775*, Oxford University Press.

Olson, A. G. (1979) Parliament, the London lobbies, and provincial interests in England and America, *Historical Reflections*, 6, 367–386.

Ormerod, H. A. (1952) Extracts from the private ledger of Arthur Heywood of Liverpool, merchant and banker, *Transactions of the Historic Society of Lancashire and Cheshire*, 103, 103–111.

Pearson, R and Richardson, R. (2001) Business networking in the industrial revolution, *Economic History Review*, 54, 657–679.

Peet, H. (1912) *Liverpool Vestry Books 1681–1834*, London University Press.

Picton, J. A. (1886) *City of Liverpool: Municipal archives and records*, Walmsley, Liverpool.

Picton, J. A. (1903) *Memorials of Liverpool: historical and topographical*, 2 vols., Walmsley, Liverpool.

Pope, D. J. (1970) *Shipping and trade in the port of Liverpool 1783–1793*, 3 vols., PhD, University of Liverpool.

Pope, D. J. (2007) The wealth and social aspirations of Liverpool's slave merchants of the second half of the eighteenth century, Chapter 7, pp 164–226, in D. Richardson, S. Schwarz and A. Tibbles (eds.) *Liverpool and transatlantic slavery*, Liverpool University Press.

Power, M. (1997) Councillors and commerce in Liverpool, 1650–1750, *Urban History*, 24, 3, 301–323.

Rathbone, E. A. (1913) *Records of the Rathbone family*, R. and R. Clark, Edinburgh.

Redford, A. (1934) *Manchester Merchants and Foreign Trade 1794–1858*, Manchester University Press.

Rees, J. S. (1949) John Phillips and Smalls Lighthouses, Part 2, *Transactions of the Historic Society of Lancashire and Cheshire*, 100, 107–118

Roberts, H. D. (1909) *Hope Street Church Liverpool*, Liverpool Booksellers Co.

Rodger, N. A. M. (2004) The Command of the Ocean: A naval history of Britain, 1649–1815, Allen Lane, London.

Sanderson, F. E. (1972) The Liverpool delegates and Sir William Dolben's Bill, *Transactions of the Historic Society of Lancashire and Cheshire*, 124, 57–84.

Sanderson, F. E. (1977) The structure of politics in Liverpool 1780–1807, *Transactions of the Historic Society of Lancashire and Cheshire*, 127, 65–88.

Sanderson, F. E. (1989) The Liverpool abolitionists, pp.196–233 in R. Anstey and P. E. H. Hair, *Liverpool, the African Slave Trade, and abolition*, Historic Society of Lancashire and Cheshire, Occasional series Vol. 2, Liverpool.

Saxton, E. B. (1949) Early records of the Mock Corporation of Sefton, *Transactions of the Historic Society of Lancashire and Cheshire*, 100, 73–92.

Schofield, W. M. (1964) The Virginia trade of the firm of Sparling and Bolden, of Liverpool, 1788–99, *Transactions of the Historic Society of Lancashire and Cheshire*, 116, 117–165.

Smithers, H. (1825) *Liverpool, its commerce, statistics, and institutions*, Thomas Kaye, London.

Thomas, P. G. (1991) *Tea Party to independence: The third phase of the American Revolution, 1773–1776*, Clarendon Press, Oxford.

Touzeau, J. (1910) *The rise and progress of Liverpool from 1551 to 1835*, Liverpool Booksellers Co.

Troughton, T. (1810) *History of Liverpool*, William Robinson, Liverpool.

Turner, W. (1957) *The Warrington Academy*, Warrington Library and Museum Committee.

Vale, E. (1967) *The Mail-Coach men of the late Eighteenth Century*, David and Charles, Newton Abbot.

Wallace, J. (1797) *A General and descriptive history of the ancient and present state of the town of Liverpool ...*, 2nd edition, London

Webb, S. and Webb, B. (1906) *English Local Government from the Revolution to the Municipal Act*, 9 vols., Longmans, London.

Williams, G. (1897) *History of the Liverpool Privateers and Letters of Marque with an Account of the Liverpool Slave Trade 1744–1812*, Heinemann, London.

Wilson, J. F. and Popp, A. (2003a) Business networking in the industrial revolution: some comments, *Economic History Review*, 54, 355–361.

Wilson, J. F. and Popp, A. (eds.) (2003b) *Industrial clusters and regional business networks in England, 1750–1970*, Ashgate, Aldershot.

Woods, E. C. (1949) John Phillips and Smalls Lighthouses, Part 1, *Transactions of the Historic Society of Lancashire and Cheshire*, 100, 91–105.

Appendix:
Tables of chamber membership

Table A.1 List of the probable chairmen, as deduced from available sources

1774–5	John Dobson 1,5 [Thomas Smythe, Deputy chair]
1775–6	
1776–7	John Dobson 2,5
1777–8	Gill Slater 1,5 [Thomas Staniforth, Deputy chair]
1778–9	Gill Slater 5
1779–80	Gill Slater 5
1780–1	
1781–2	Gill Slater 3,5 [Thomas Staniforth, Deputy chair]
1782–3	Gill Slater 6
1783–4	
1784–5	
1785–6	
1786–7	possibly Henry Wilckens 4
1787–8	
1788–9	possibly Henry Wilckens 4
1789–90	
1790–1	possibly Edgar Corrie 4
1791–2	possibly Edgar Corrie 4
1792–3	
1793–4	possibly John Tarleton 4
1794–5	possibly John Tarleton 4
1795–6	possibly John Tarleton 4

1 Based on published newspaper reports.
2 From the Abstract of 1777.
3 From Gore's Directory 1781, the only year to list the committee.
4 Based on correspondence writing 'in the general interest'.
5 From correspondence with the Bristol Merchant Venturers.
6 From correspondence with Glasgow chamber of commerce.

Table A.2 Liverpool chamber of commerce known members, activities, markets, and type of business. The four additional members, not known as committee members, are listed at foot of table. Activities and type of business as at 1780; except Cragg and Nelson which are for 1790–3. The last column is the count of number of years on the chamber's committee over the 12 years 1774–1786. Abbreviations: I: individual mainly not trading in partnership; Co: mainly trading in partnership; mf. Manufacturing. WI: West Indies

(Sources: entries in *Williamsons* and *Gores Advertisers*, and *Manchester Mercury*; Gore's Liverpool Directory 1766 - 1790; Bailey's Northern Directory 1781; Liverpool freeman register 352 CLE/REG 1/1–2; and secondary sources, chiefly Smithers, 1825; Baines, 1852; Aspinall, 1852; Brooke, 1853; Boardman, 1871; Fox Bourne, 1886; Williams, 1897; Hughes, 1906; Rathbone, 1913; Boney, 1957; Barker and Harris, 1959; Schofield, 1964; Pope, 1970, 2007; Craig and Jarvis, 1967; Hyde, 1971; Behrendt, 1990; Littler, 1996; Haggerty, 2006; Morgan, 2007; Liverpool RO, and entries at TNA; John Tarleton's account books LRO 920 TAR 2/22–6; slaving from same sources, and for 1789–91 from *Brynes Merchant Networks: British Slavers of 1789*, web source).

Name	Activity	Markets	Type of business	Chamber role
John Armstrong	Merchant		I	1
Nicholas Ashton	Major salt merchant exporting to America and ship-owner; St. Helens and Dungeon salt works mf.; coal mining and salt at St. Helens (with George Case)	America and UK	I also Co.	6
Robert Bent	Merchant and shipping, slaving (with Ellis Bent)	Africa and WI	I also Co.	1
William Bolden	Merchant and ship-owner; some slaving	America (Virginia)	I also Co.	9
John Bolton	Major merchant, Esq., slaving, ship-owner (with Staniforth, Brooks, Slater, Ryan)	WI	I also Co.	1
Joseph Brooks jun	Merchant and major ship-owner (with Ingram, Staniforth, Carruthers, Slater, Ryan), slaving, turpentine merchant, rope mf., brewing	America	Co.	11
Charles Caldwell	Sugar baker mf, merchant (with Matthews and Wallace) (major banker and also ship-owner with Smythe)	UK and America	I also Co.	3
James Carruthers	Merchant, major corn trader, ship-owner (with Brooks, Ingram, Staniforth, Heywood), slaving, copper smelting	Mainly Africa also Europe	Co.	3
Thomas Case	Merchant, shipping, slaving (with Dobson), colliery, coal agent (with Gregson and Clayton), glass mf, real estate, plantation owner (later prtnr in Gregsons bank)	São Tomé, Africa, America	Co.	4

Name	Activity	Markets	Type of business	Chamber role
Edward Chaffers	Merchant, glass and pottery mf (mugs), some slaving	UK and America	Co.	10
John Chorley	Merchant and ship-owner of Lancaster (with Rawlinson and Wallace), sugar store, also tanning	America, UK	Co.	10
John Copland	Merchant		I	1
Edgar Corrie	Beer brewer, corn factor (with Robert Greenham, Roscoe and Gladstone)	UK, Europe, America	I also Co.	5
Joseph Dalterra	Merchant (with Dobson; Ryan; Walker), slaving, banking (1791– with Ingram, Goore, Staniforth and Bold); bankrupt with Dobson 1778, soon refloated	Africa and WI	Co.	3
John Dobson	Major merchant (with Dalterra; Walker; Rob. Nicholson; Thos Hodgson; Henry Hulton), corn dealer and provisions to Europe, whaling, slaving (with Case); also joint investor with Josia Wedgwood in Reid & Co china warehouse; bankrupt with Dalterra 1778	WI and Africa, Europe	I also Co.	8
George Dunbar	Major shipping (with Halliday) and major insurance broker and cotton merchant (with George Hall, linen and ruffia merchant)	Europe, America	I also Co.	1
William Earle	Major merchant, packet service to Leghorn, major ship-owner (with Thos Hodgson, Ingram and Leyland) (and slaving with brother Thos) also ironmonger and anchorsmith; later coal mining	WI, Africa, Leghorn and Mediterranean, Amsterdam	Co.	1
Edward Falkner	Merchant and slaving	Africa, America	Co.	1
Thomas Falkner	Merchant (with A. Heywood), major slaving	N. Carolina	Co.	3
John Fisher	Major ship-owner, ship builder and merchant, some slaving	Africa	I	3
Joseph Fowden	Merchant, ship-owner and slaving, Gent.	Africa, America	Co.	1
Thomas Foxcroft	Merchant and slaving, from Lancaster	America, WI, Africa	Co.	7
Samuel Halliday	Merchant and linen trader, major ship-owner	Africa, America and Ireland	Co.	1
Stephen Hayes	Merchant and timber trader, coastal shipping (possibly part of Campbell and George Hayes & Co., major ship-owners and merchants; or Hayes Wm & Co, pot warehouse)	America and Ireland	I and Co.	1

Name	Activity	Markets	Type of business	Chamber role
Arthur Heywood	Major ship-owner, slaving (with Thos. Falkner), merchant, major banking (with Benjamin)	America, WI, Africa, UK	Co.	8
Benjamin Heywood	Major ship-owner, slaving (with Thos. Falkner), merchant, major banking (with Arthur); also glassworks (with Staniforth)	America, WI, Africa, UK	Co.	4
Richard Heywood	Banking (with Arthur), insurance; 1783– hotel proprietor (with Slater, Gregson and Ryan)	America, WI, Africa	Co.	3
John Hodgson	Ship-owner (with other Hodgsons), merchant, major slaving	Africa, America	Co.	7
Thomas Hodgson	Merchant, shipping (with other Hodgsons), and insurance broker (with son), also sugar refining (with Black, Blundell, Sparling et al.)	America, Bahamas, Senegal, Leghorn	I also Co.	4
Thomas Hodgson jun	Merchant, shipping (with other Hodgsons), and insurance broker (with father),major slaving, (probable supporter of slave trade abolition)	America	Co.	8
Francis Ingram	Merchant in tar and pitch, ship-owner (with Earle, Leyland, Staniforth), slaving, banker (1791– with Earle, Dalterra, Goore and Bold, later with Staniforth), rope mf, copperas mf. (ferrous sulphate)	Africa, America	Co.	3
William James	Major cattle merchant, broker, major ship-owner, slaving	Africa, Guinea, America	I	2
John Kennion jun	Merchant and major ship-owner; grain merchant	Africa, America	I also Co.	2
Richard Kent	Timber and general merchant and ship-owner and builder, salt mf. at Northwich, white lead mf., Winsford flats agent 1767–74	America	I	11
Thomas Lake	Merchant and Irish shipping packet service (with William); potter (with William and Richard); later slaving	UK, Ireland	Co.	5

Name	Activity	Markets	Type of business	Chamber role
William Charles Lake	Merchant and Irish shipping packet service (with Thomas); potter (with Thomas and Richard); later slaving	UK, Ireland	Co.	3
Joseph Leay	Merchant, earthenware warehouse	UK, America	Co.	1
Hugh Hindley Leigh	Merchant and ship-owner	Africa	Co.	2
Thomas Leyland	Major merchant, ship-owner (with Earle and Ingram; later with Tuoy), Irish meat and provisions; olive oil, wine, major slaving, later banking (with Clarke and Roscoe)	Africa, America, Ireland, Europe, Spain	Co.	3
Thomas Manley	Wine merchant	Europe	I also Co.	1
Edward Mason	Grain merchant, provisions and ship-owner, slaving	Africa, America and Ireland	Co.	1
Arnold Meyer	Linen merchant and shipping (some with Wilckens)	Africa, America	Co.	2
John Myers	Corn merchant (with Trotter)	America, UK and Europe	Co.	2
Matthew Nicholson	Linen and textiles merchant and shipping (with various other Nicholsons); copperas works (Paisley and Wigan) (1788 banker with Heywoods in Manchester)	WI and America	Co.	1
Alexander Nottingham	Merchant and major ship-owner (with son), slaving	Africa, America	Co.	6
Joseph Rathbone	Timber merchant; also brewing, earthenware, glass, soap, salt and coal	America	Co.	1
Thos Henry Rawlinson	Merchant and ship-owner (with Chorley), in Lancaster and Liverpool, sugar store	America and West Indies	Co.	7
Thomas Rawson	Merchant		Co.	1
Thomas Ryan	Wine merchant, linen trader, major broker (also slaving with Dalterrra), ship-owner (with Brooks, Slater, Bolton, Staniforth); of Montserrat in 1776 (payments from John Tarleton); 1783– hotel proprietor (with Slater, Gregson and Heywood)	Africa, America, WI, Europe	I also Co.	3
Gill (Gilbert) Slater	Major provision merchant and ship-owner, insurance, slaving; 1783– hotel proprietor (with Gregson, Heywood and Ryan)	America, Grenada, St. Vincent, Africa	I also Co.	12
Thomas Smythe	Major merchant, also banker and ship-owner (with Caldwell)	UK	I also Co.	9

Name	Activity	Markets	Type of business	Chamber role
Thomas Staniforth	Major ship-owner, Greenland fisheries (with Charles Goore), merchant, banker (1791– with Dalterra, Ingram, Bold), major slaving, real estate; rope mf., glassworks (with B. Heywood)	Africa, America; also Europe, Greenland and Canada	Co.	12
John Tarleton	Sugar baker & merchant (with Thomas), major ship-owner (with Brooks, Backhouse etc.), whaling, major slaving	Curacao and Grenada, Greenland	Co.	1
Thomas Tarleton	Merchant and ship-owner (with John Backhouse and others), sugar refining, major slaving, insurance	WI estates	Co.	5
Tyzack Trotter	Corn merchant (with Myers)	America	Co.	1
George Venables	Linen, sugar and general merchant	Jamaica, America	I	9
Benedict Paul Wagner	Merchant, shipping, shipping agent (and merchant with Armstrong and Taylor); later Venetian consul at Liverpool	America, Europe	Co.	1
William Wallace	Grain merchant, provisions merchant (with Carruthers); shipping (with Chorley and Rawlinson)	Africa, Ireland	I also Co.	9
Richard Watt jun	Merchant, shipping and WI estates (with uncle), rope mf. (with George Green)	WI	Co.	7
Henry Wilckens	Shipping (with Meyer); Cheshire salt mf. and general merchant/dealer	America and UK	Co.	1
Samuel Green (Sec)	Merchant, mainly linen	America and Ireland	I	N/a
John Cragg	Merchant, iron founder and soap manufacture	UK	I also Co.	N/a
Ambrose Lace	Merchant and shipping captain, wine, slaving (with Roscoe and Aspinall)	Africa, America, Iberia	Co.	N/a
Jacob Nelson	Merchant, shipping; 'Merchants Counting House' (with Pearson)	UK, America	Co.	N/a
John Walker	Major merchant (with Dobson & Dalterra; some with Richard Watt's uncle) and shipping captain, slaving	Africa, America, Europe	I and Co.	N/a

Table A.3 Activities, markets and type of business (as at 1780) of the 23 additional 'probable' members of the Liverpool Chamber of Commerce in 1775: derived from Benjamin Heywood's *Curious Papers*, and the same sources as Appendix Table A.2

Name	Activity	Markets	Type of business
Appleton Samuel	Provisions merchant	Ireland and UK	I
Backhouse Daniel	Merchant, provisions and major ship-owner (with Tarleton and others), slaving	America, West Indies, Africa, Ireland	Co.
Black Patrick	Shipping capt. for Whalley & Co., and merchant; sugar baker (with Blundell, Hodgson, Sparling et al.), slaving	Africa and America	Co.
Blundell Jonathan	Major merchant, sugar baker (with Black, Hodgson, Sparling et al.), (later canal proprietor with Wm. Earle, Chaffers etc), slaving	Africa, WI and UK	Co
Bootle William	Merchant		Co.
Grayson Anthony	Timber merchant, shipping capt. and ship builder (with Foster Cunliffe)	America and WI	I and Co.
Gregson John	Boatman in Customs; merchant; later receiver of taxes for Lancashire	UK	N/a
Grime Richard	Merchant		Co.
Grimshaw Robert	Provisions, slaving, capt., from Lancaster	America, Gold Coast, WI	Co.
Hesketh William	Major ship-owner (with brother Robt), merchant, pottery mf.	Africa	Co
Holland Nehemiah	Merchant and pottery mf., capt.	America	I
Jones John Chambres	Merchant, slaving	Africa	I
Kelly Samuel	Merchant (with brother Thomas)		Co

Name	Activity	Markets	Type of business
Kewley Philip	Merchant (with John and Patrick Kewley)	Grenada and WI	Co.
Mason William	Tobacco merchant, shipping and sales	America	Co.
Mears William M.	Merchant, wine trade	Mediterranean	Co
Ormandy William	Bookseller	UK	I
Parke Thomas	Linen merchant, shipping (with Ingram, Carruthers, Dennison, Heywoods etc.), later bank with Tuoy, Gregson, Morland etc.); fire insurance with Heywoods etc.; slaving	America	Co.
Parker John	Merchant (with Tarletons and others), slaving	America	Co.
Shaw John.	Merchant, insurance broker with father Samuel, slaving	Africa and UK	Co
Spe(y)ers William	Capt. and ship-owner (with Tuoy), slaving (with Thomas Speers, Tuoy, et al.)	Africa, America	Co.
Tuohy David	Capt. and ship-owner, slaving (with Heywoods, Speers; later with Leyland), Irish provisions, later bank (with Ingram, Dennison and Parke etc.)	Africa	I and Co.
Weatherherd Christopher	Merchant, broker	America	Co

Table A.4 Chamber of commerce known members, birth and death dates (where known), religion, and involvement with other organisations and societies; foot of table percentages of those alive at the time; indicates known to be dead, not in Liverpool at this date, or under 20; a space indicates not a member; c indicates a member of the committee

Joseph Brooks junior is ascribed to being Anglican because his father and son were; indeed his son became archdeacon and then rector of Liverpool. His uncle was Joseph Brooks, treasurer of the vestry and member of many other organisations, who subscribed to several dissenter activities, but this seems to have been to support their works, as there is no record of the Brooks family being active dissenters. A plaque of tribute to him in the Paradise St. chapel (for his 'exertions for the welfare of the town ... and relief of the poor': Roberts, 1909, p 512; see also Brooke, 1853; Pope, 1970) demonstrates the regard in which he was held, but he has no other evidenced relationship with the chapel. + William Wallace was reputedly Catholic, but has not been found in local Catholic records, although someone of that name is nonconformist.

Sources: Birth and death dates from DNB, newspaper reports, Freeman Registers, International Genealogical Index (IGI) etc.; Corporation Freemen up to 1784 from LRO 352 CLE/REG 1/1, and poll books for 1761 and 1784; Africa Company Freemen from TNA T 70/1508, and LRO 352 MD 1, Committee Book, also listings of the committee in Wakefield's and other national directories; deaths, plus Evans, 1887, Roberts, 1909, from same sources as births and deaths. A=Anglican; C=Catholic; D=Dissenters; from same sources as births and deaths, plus Evans, 1887, Roberts, 1909, and records of dissenting chapels TNA BMD records, RG 4, 6 etc.; Unanimous Society members 1753–78 from LRO 367 UNA/1; Ugly Face Society 1743–57 from LRO 367 UGL 1/1; Sefton Mock Corporation 1753 –90 from LRO 367 SEF 1 and 2: Subscription Library members 1769–92 from LRO 027 LYC 1/1/1, 1/1/2 and 3/1; Athenaeum membership in 1797 from Carrick and Ashton, 1997, Appendix 2.

Name	Birth/ death	Relig	Freeman Corpn.	Freeman Africa Co.	Unan. Soc.	Ugly face Soc	Sefton Corpn.	Subs. library	Athenaeum
John Armstrong	1738–	D/A	•					•	
Nicholas Ashton	1742–1833	D/A	•			–	•	•c	•
Robert Bent	1744–1831	D		•		–			
William Bolden	1730–1800	A	•					•	
John Bolton	1756–1837	A				–			•
Joseph Brooks jun.	1746–1823	A*	•	•	•	–		•c	•
Charles Caldwell	1739–1814	A	•			–	•	•c	–
James Carruthers	c.1718	D/A		•		–	•	•	•
Thomas Case	1731–	A		•					
Edward Chaffers	1734–1810	A	•			–		•c	•
John Chorley	c.1735–c1810	D	•		•c	–	•	•	
John Copland	1727–	D					•	•	
Edgar Corrie	–1819	D/A		•				•	

Name	Birth/death	Relig	Freeman Corpn.	Freeman Africa Co.	Unan. Soc.	Ugly face Soc	Sefton Corpn.	Subs. library	Athenaeum
Joseph Dalterra	c.1732–1793	D					•	•c	-
John Dobson	?1729–91	D	•?				•		-
George Dunbar	c.1749–1811	A	•			-	•	•	•
William Earle	1721–88	A	•	•			•	•	-
Edward Falkner	1750–1825	A	•			-	•	•	•
Thomas Falkner	1719–85	A	•				•	•	-
John Fisher	1740–91	A	•			-		•	-
Joseph Fowden	c.1740–	A				-	•	•	
Thomas Foxcroft	1733–1809	A	•		•	-	•	•	
Samuel Halliday	1748–	D	•			-		•c	
Stephen Hayes	1732–	D	•			-	•	•	
Arthur Heywood	1717–95	D	•	•				•	-
Benjamin Heywood	1723–95	D	•	•		•		•c	-
Richard Heywood	1751–1800	D	•			-		•	•
John Hodgson	1736–1813	D	•	•		-		•	
Thomas Hodgson	1729–1823	D	•	•		•	•	•	•
Thomas Hodgson jun	1739–1817	D	•	•	•	-			•
Francis Ingram	1739–1815	A	•	•		-			-
William James	1734–98	A	•			-		•	
John Kennion jun	1725–81	D	•	•		•		•c	-
Richard Kent	1745–	A	•		•	-	•	•	
Thomas Lake	c.1745–	A	•			-	•		
William Charles Lake	1753–1836	A	•			-			•
Joseph Leay	c.1746–	A				-		•	•
Hugh Hindley Leigh	?1738–79	A				-			-
Thomas Leyland	1752–1827	A?	•			-	•		•
Thomas Manley	c.1760–	A	•			-	•		

Name	Birth/death	Relig	Freeman Corpn.	Freeman Africa Co.	Unan. Soc.	Ugly face Soc	Sefton Corpn.	Subs. library	Athenaeum
Edward Mason	1735–1814	A				-		•	
Arnold Meyer		A						•	
John Myers	?1727–	A					•	•	-
Matthew Nicholson	1759–1849	D	•		-	-		•	-
Alexander Nottingham	1737–81	A	•	•	•	-	•		-
Joseph Rathbone	1746–c.93	D	•			-		•c	-
Thos Henry Rawlinson	1743–86	A	•		•	-	•		-
Thomas Rawson	?1734–c.1815	A				-	•		•
Thomas Ryan	1738–1802	A	•	•		-	•		•
Gill (Gilbert) Slater	1737–1802	A	•	•		-	•	•c	
Thomas Smythe	1737–1824	A	•			-	•	•c	•
Thomas Staniforth	1735–1803	A	•	•		-		•c	•
John Tarleton	1755–1841	A	•	•		-		•	
Thomas Tarleton	1753–1820	A	•	•	•	-			•
Tyzack Trotter	?1750–	A?				-			
George Venables	1720–	A			•	-	•	•	•
Benedict Paul Wagner	c.1730–	D					•		
William Wallace+	c.1745–	C/D				-		•c	
Richard Watt jun	c.1740–1801	A				-	•	•	•
Henry Wilckens (arr. Lpool 1767)	1751–1821	D?						•	•
Samuel Green (Sec)	1728–92	D?						•	-
John Cragg	1767–1854	A				-	•	•	
Ambrose Lace	1727–94	A	•		-		•	•c	-
Jacob Nelson	c.1735–	D				-	•	•	
John Walker	?1747–	D?	•			-	•	•	•
Total no.	-	A=c.43 (max)	39	19	9	3	30	46	20
% of chamber members	-	A=64.6 (max)	60.0	29.2	14.3	15.8	46.2	70.8	42.6

Table A.5 Probable members of the chamber, and their affiliation; • indicates their affiliation; indicates known to be dead or left area at this date, or under 20; a space indicates not a member; c indicates a member of the committee.   Sources: as in Table A.3

Name	Birth/ death	Relig	Freeman Corpn.	Freeman Africa Co.	Unan Soc.	Ugly face Soc	Sefton Corpn.	Subs. library	Athenaeum
Samuel Appleton	?1740–	A	•					•	
Daniel Backhouse	1741–1811	A	•			-	•		
Patrick Black	1728–1816	A		•				•	
Jonathan Blundell	c.1723–1800	A	•	•			•	•	
William Bootle	?1738–	D				-			
Anthony Grayson	1719–85	A							-
John Gregson	1755–1802	A?	•			-			•
Richard Grime	?1702–	A?							
Robert Grimshaw	1720–81	D?					•	•	-
William Hesketh	?1717–	A?	•					•	
Nehemiah Holland	1713–86	A	•				•		-
John Chambres Jones	1715–1833	A		•			•	•	
Samuel Kelly	c.1730–	A							
Philip Kewley	c.1740–c.1800	A				-			
William Mason	1740–	A	•			-	•		
William Marshall Mears	1750–	A				-		•	
William Ormandy	1751–	D				-	•		
Thomas Parke	1729–1819	D	•	•			•	•c	•

Name	Birth/death	Relig	Freeman Corpn.	Freeman Africa Co.	Unan Soc.	Ugly face Soc	Sefton Corpn.	Subs. library	Athenaeum
John Parker	1740–95	A/C				-	•		-
John Shaw	1743–1807	A	•	•		-			•
William Spe(y)ers	1755–	A				-			
David Tuohy	1734–88	A				-			-
Christopher Weatherherd	1726– c.1795	A							
Total no	23	A=19 (max)	9	6	0	0	9	8	3
% of probable members	-	A=82.6 (max)	39.1	26.1	0	0	39.1	34.8	17.6

Table A.6. Known members of Liverpool chamber of commerce signing petitions 1762–80. The Dunbars were brothers trading in partnership; – indicates known to be under 20 at that date (but those under 20 actually signing are included)

Name	1762 paper money	Stamp Act 1765	Stamp Act thanks 1766	Docks 1766	Wilkes 1769	Free ports 1773	Peace 1775	Loyal 1775	Offices 1780
John Armstrong	•						•		
Nicholas Ashton		•			•	•		•	
Robert Bent	–								
William Bolden						•		•	•
John Bolton	–	–	–	–	–	–		–	
Joseph Brooks jun	sen.	sen.	•	sen.		•		•	
Charles Caldwell		•	•	•	•	•	•		•
James Carruthers		•	•					•	•
Thomas Case				•	•				
Edward Chaffers		•							
John Chorley		•		•		•	•		
John Copland					•				
Edgar Corrie						•			
Joseph Dalterra		•	•	•	•	•	•	•	
John Dobson		•	•	•	•	•	•		
George Dunbar	Thos	•		Thos		Thos			•
William Earle		•	•	•		•		•	
Edward Falkner	–	–	–	–	–	•			
Thomas Falkner		•	•	•	•				
John Fisher				•	•			•	
Joseph Fowden									
Thomas Foxcroft			•	•	•	•			•
Samuel Halliday	–	•		•	•		•		

Name	1762 paper money	Stamp Act 1765	Stamp Act thanks 1766	Docks 1766	Wilkes 1769	Free ports 1773	Peace 1775	Loyal 1775	Offices 1780
Stephen Hayes		•	•	•			•		
Arthur Heywood	•	•	•	•		•	•		•
Benjamin Heywood	•	•	•	•		•	•		•
Richard Heywood	–	–	–	–	–		•		•
John Hodgson									
Thomas Hodgson		•	•	•	•	•	•		
Thomas Hodgson jun			•	•					•
Francis Ingram		•	•	•		•			
William James			•		•	•	•		•
John Kennion jun		•	•	•	•	•		•	
Richard Kent	–	•	•	•	•	•	•		
Thomas Lake				–	–	•	•		
William Charles Lake	–	–	–	–	–				
Joseph Leay	–	–						•	•
Hugh Hindley Leigh								•	
Thomas Leyland+	–	–	–	–	–	•		•	•
Thomas Manley	–	–	–	–	–	–	–	•	
Edward Mason						•			
Arnold Meyer					•	•		•	
John Myers					•			•	
Matthew Nicholson	–	–		–	–	–	•		
Alexander Nottingham		•	•			•			•
Joseph Rathbone	–	–	–						
Thos Henry Rawlinson		•		•		•	•		
Thomas Rawson									

Name	1762 paper money	Stamp Act 1765	Stamp Act thanks 1766	Docks 1766	Wilkes 1769	Free ports 1773	Peace 1775	Loyal 1775	Offices 1780
Thomas Ryan									•
Gill (Gilbert) Slater							•		
Thomas Smythe		•	•	•	•	•			
Thomas Staniforth	•	•	•	•	•	•			•
John Tarleton	sen	-	-	-	•			•	•
Thomas Tarleton	-	-	-	-	-			•	•
Tyzack Trotter									
George Venables						•			•
Benedict Paul Wagner		-	•						•
William Wallace	-		•	•	•		•		
Richard Watt jun						-	•		
Henry Wilckens	-	-	-	-	-	-		•	
Samuel Green (Sec)					•		•		
John Cragg	-				-		-	-	
Ambrose Lace			•	-	-	-	-	•	•
Jacob Nelson								•	•
John Walker	•	•	•	•	•		•	•	•
Chamber names	8	23	25	25	22	27	21	19	22
No. over 20	49	51	53	54	55	60	62	63	64
% of members signing	16.3	45.1	47.2	46.3	40.0	45.0	33.9	30.2	34.4
Known + probable signing	10	28	30	31	24	29	21	42	32
% of all members signing	14.9	40.6	42.3	41.9	32.0	35.8	24.4	48.3	36.8
Total petition names	32	115	164	88	1113	55	215	470	177
Known + probable as % of all names	31.3	24.3	18.3	35.2	2.2	52.7	9.8	8.9	18.1

Table A.7 Probable members of Liverpool chamber of commerce signing petitions 1762–80. Some names substituted where known to be closely related in their business; – indicates known to be under 20 at that date

Name	1762 paper money	Stamp Act 1765	Stamp Act thanks 1766	Docks 1766	Wilkes 1769	Free ports 1773	Peace 1775	Loyal 1775	Offices 1780
Samuel Appleton								•	•
Daniel Backhouse	John			John				•	•
Patrick Black		•						•	•
Jonathan Blundell	•	•		•				•	•
William Bootle								•	
Anthony Grayson								•	
John Gregson	–	–	–	–	–			•	•
Richard Grime								•	
Robert Grimshaw								•	
William Hesketh	Robt.	Robt.	Robt.	Robt.		Robt.		•	•
Nehemiah Holland		•	•		•			•	
John Chambres Jones	–	–	–	–	–	–		•	
Samuel Kelly	–	Thos.	•					•	
Philip Kewley								•	
William Mason								•	
William M. Mears	–	–	–	•				•	•
William Ormandy	–	–	–	–	–			•	

Name	1762 paper money	Stamp Act 1765	Stamp Act thanks 1766	Docks 1766	Wilkes 1769	Free ports 1773	Peace 1775	Loyal 1775	Offices 1780
Thomas Parke			•		•			•	
John Parker			•					•	•
John Shaw				Sam.		Sam.		•	
William Spe(y)ers	-	-	-	-	-	-		•	
David Tuohy								•	•
Chris Weatherherd				•		•		•	•
Chamber names	2	5	5	6	2	2	0	23	10
No. aged over 20	18	18	18	20	20	21	23	23	23
% of probable	11.1	27.7	27.7	30.0	10.0	9.5	0	100	43.5

Table A.8 Members of Liverpool Corporation's Committee of Trade signing petitions 1762–80. In 1775 two Thomas Golightlys sign, but it is not certain that either is the member of the committee; Thomas Staniforth is a chamber member included in earlier tables; – indicates known to be under 20 at that date; percentage calculated from those over 20 at time

Name	1762 paper money	Stamp Act 1765	Stamp Act thanks 1766	Docks 1766	Wilkes 1769	Free ports 1773	Peace 1775	Loyal 1775	Offices 1780
John Blackburne jun				•					
John Brown	•	•	•	•		•	•	•	
George Case	-	-	-	-		•		•	•
William Crosbie sen		•	•	•				•	•
William Crosbie jun	-	-				•		•	•
Thomas Earle	-	-	-	-	-	-		•	•
John Greenwood									
John Gregson	-	-	-	-	-	-		•	•
William Gregson	•	•		•	-	•		•	•
Thomas Golightly			•			•	(•)	•	•
Charles Pole								•	
William Roe									
John Shaw	•	•	•	•	•	•		•	•
(Thomas Staniforth)	-	-	-	-	-	-			
Clayton Tarleton						-	-	-	-
Committee names signing	3	4	3	5	1	6	(1)	9	8
% of committee signing	33.3	40.0	27.3	45.5	8.3	50.0	(8.3)	75.5	66.7

Index

Note on the index:
Some of the terms indexed apply to the footnotes as well as the main text, so may be found in both on a particular page; numbers in *italics* indicate the presence of a person in a table, while **bold** numerals denote a photograph.

Photo credits

Cover images: 1786 Yates map of Lancashire
Courtesy of Lancashire Record Office, Lancashire County Council

1771 Bonne map of East coast America
Courtesy of mapsofpa.com

Back cover: Liverpool, 1768 Eyer
Courtesy of Liverpool Record Office, Central Library, Liverpool

Page 5:   Draft article to establish the chamber
Holt Gregson Papers
Courtesy of Liverpool Record Office, Central Library, Liverpool
Ref: HOL 10 p. 355

Page 11:   Advertisement for the Tontine hotel (Bates)
Courtesy of Liverpool Record Office, Central Library, Liverpool
Ref: HOL 18 p.127

Page 16:   Arthur Heywood
Courtesy of Barclays Group Archive, Manchester

Page 19:   Newspaper advert for the AGM
From: Williamsons Advertiser, 1777
Courtesy of Liverpool Record Office, Central Library, Liverpool

Page 26:   The abstract of the chamber's first three years
Courtesy of the Athenaeum Archive, copyright Athenaeum Liverpool

Page 27:   Letter from chamber president John Dobson, 1777
Courtesy of Bristol Record Office
Ref: SMV 2/4/2/20(15)

Page 78:   Liverpool, 1768 Eyer
Courtesy of Liverpool Record Office, Central Library, Liverpool

Page 89:   Heywoods bank, Castle Street, late 1790s
From: Four centuries of banking
Chandler, George; 1964
Courtesy of Barclays Group Archive, Manchester

Page 104:   Matthew Nicholson,
Courtesy of Liverpool Record Office, Central Library, Liverpool
Richard Heywood
Courtesy of Barclays Group Archive, Manchester